THE
REFERENCE
SHELF

ENGLISH:

OUR OFFICIAL LANGUAGE?

Edited by BEE GALLEGOS

THE REFERENCE SHELF

Volume 66 Number 2

THE H. W. WILSON COMPANY

New York   1994

THE REFERENCE SHELF

The books in this series contain reprints of articles, excerpts from books, and addresses on current issues and social trends in the United States and other countries. There are six separately bound numbers in each volume, all of which are generally published in the same calendar year. One number is a collection of recent speeches; each of the others is devoted to a single subject and gives background information and discussion from various points of view, concluding with a comprehensive bibliography that contains books and pamphlets and abstracts of additional articles on the subject. Books in the series may be purchased individually or on subscription.

Library of Congress Cataloging-in-Publication Data

English—our official language? / edited by Bee Gallegos.
  p. cm. — (The Reference shelf ; v. 66, no. 2)
  Includes bibliographical references.
  ISBN 0-8242-0857-9
  1. Language policy—United States. 2. English language—United States. 3. Language and education—United States. I. Gallegos, Bee. II. Series.
P119.32.U6E54 1994
306.4'4973—dc20   94-7872
                                                         CIP

Cover: The growing immigrant population of many U.S. cities has prompted newsstand owners to increase the number of foreign-language publications they sell.

Photo: AP/Wide World Photos

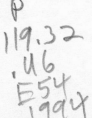

P
119.32
.U6
E54
1994

Printed in the United States of America

CONTENTS

III. Social, Cultural, and Economic Implications

IV. Education and Official English

PREFACE

Many Americans assume that English is the official language of the United States, but while the majority of U.S. citizens speak English as their first or second language, and it is the language of our laws, constitution, and government, there is nothing in the U.S. Constitution that gives English preference over any other language. The framers of the Constitution were silent on this issue; in fact, the omission of the matter in Madison's notes seems to indicate that the question of a national language never came up at the Federal Convention. The view at the time may have been that non-English-speaking immigrants would assimilate without the coercion of language.

The controversy over establishing English as the official language, however, is not a new one. The conditions contributing to the most recent official-language movement have been present in the United States through most of its history, and the arguments for and against have been repeated time and again with little variation. One of the arguments most often presented in favor of an official language considers how much diversity a nation can tolerate. Another argument is based on nationalism and claims that speaking a language other than English is "un-American" and that assimilation of new immigrants would happen much more quickly if everyone was forced to "sink or swim" in the waters of the English language. The most recent resurgence of the issue began in 1981 with the introduction of legislation by the late United States Senator S. I. Hayakawa. His legislation, calling for an amendment to the U.S. Constitution that would declare English the official language of the nation, was not passed.

For opponents of the establishment of English as the nation's official language, equal access to education and government and the right to speak the language of one's choice are the major tenets. Indeed, research now shows that today's immigrants are learning the language of their new country at the same pace as those of previous generations: the immigrant continues to speak his or her first language, acquiring little knowledge of English; the second generation begins the transition by becoming bilingual, often speaking one language at home and another at school or work. The third generation makes the shift to the almost exclusive use of the English language and retain little knowledge of the language of their ancestors.

The articles in this compilation have been selected to provide different views of an issue that has arisen throughout the history of the United States. Section one examines the English only question from all sides and contains arguments for and against from the leading two organizations: U.S. English (for) and the English Plus Information Clearinghouse (against).

Section two outlines the history of language controversy in the United States, including the political debates and legal causes.

The articles in section three discuss the issues of language acquisition, assimilation, and cultural identity, as well as the role of language in the workplace.

Section four deals with the impact of the language controversy on the educational system, particularly on bilingual education programs.

The editor is indebted to the authors and publishers who have granted permission for these materials to be reprinted in this compilation. Special appreciation is due to Vicki Eppich, who proofed my writing and provided support in many ways, and to my daughter Jamie, for her patience. Lastly, I wish to thank Lee for saying all the right things when I needed encouragement.

Bee Gallegos

March 1994

I. ENGLISH ONLY VS. ENGLISH PLUS: AN OVERVIEW OF THE DEBATE

EDITOR'S INTRODUCTION

The question of whether there should be an official language in the United States is a debater's dream topic. Strong feelings are present on both sides of this issue. Proponents see official language legislation as a matter of patriotism and national unity, while detractors see it as taking away the right to free speech as well as destroying a cultural heritage. The articles in this section attempt to educate the reader about what the official English controversy means in its current incarnation. The first article appeared in *EPIC Events,* the newsletter of the English Plus Information Clearinghouse (EPIC), an organization established in 1983 that opposes official-language legislation but favors strong English-language proficiency *plus* mastery of a second or even multiple languages. The article charts the course of the official English debate through the decade of the 1980s. Although both authors represent organizations supportive of English Plus, their article is straightforward and factual.

The following two articles support the official-English movement and passage of the English Language Amendment (ELA). The first, a speech by the late S. I. Hayakawa from 1985 and later published as a pamphlet *English Language Amendment: One Nation . . . Indivisible?* discusses the reason he believed that an amendment to the constitution was crucial. A linguist and founder of U.S. English, Hayakawa argued that a common language is the glue that keeps American society together. The third article presents the views of U.S. English, the leading organization pushing for the passage of official-language legislation.

In opposition to the ELA is the "Statement of Purpose" from English Plus Information Clearinghouse.

The final article in this section is a summary of the pros and cons of the English-language debate by Leah Eskin and reprinted from *Scholastic Update.*

9

LANGUAGE DEBATES IN THE UNITED STATES[1]

Not since the beginning of the century has language received as much attention in the United States as it did during the 1980s. Like the early 1900s, the language battles of the 1980s were rife with appeals to patriotism and unity, casting language minorities in the role of outsiders or foreigners who deliberately "chose" not to learn the English language.

Unlike the 1900s, when language issues were confined primarily to local and state arenas, those of the 1980s have been orchestrated at the national level by a powerful and highly funded political organization. Ostensibly, the whole purpose of this organization is to establish English as the official language of the United States, but its connections to restrictionist, anti-immigration organizations suggest a wider, more far-reaching agenda.

The irony of the appearance of the English-only movement in the 1980s is that it calls for a return to a mythic era of English monolingualism in the face of the reality of our growing multilingual, multicultural population and the economic demands of multilingual ability in the world market.

Setting the Stage

As the nation prepared to enter the 1980s, two states had measures on the books declaring English the official language. Nebraska's constitutional amendment dated back to 1923, when the country was experiencing a wave of anti-German sentiment because of World War I. Illinois' 1969 statute amended a 1923 law which had declared "American" the state's official language.

The President's Commission on Foreign Language and International Studies had just released its report on the "scandalous" lack of foreign language ability on the part of Americans. Not one state required foreign language study for high school graduation. Many states did not even require schools to offer foreign language study.

[1]Article by Jamie B. Draper, JNCL and Martha Jimenez, MALDEF. From *Epic Events* 2(5): 1,4,7, '90. Copyright © 1990 by National Immigration, Refugee & Citizenship Forum. Reprinted with permission.

The 1970s also ushered in an era of close scrutiny of the Bilingual Education Act following the 1974 *Lau vs. Nichols* Supreme Court ruling requiring schools to offer special assistance to limited-English proficient students. The 1978 amendments to the Bilingual Education Act emphasized that the goal of the law was to achieve competence in the English language. Programs funded under Title VII would be transitional only; no funds would be made available for native language maintenance.

The stage was set for a decade of debate on language in American society.

1980

• Dade County, Florida voters approve an anti-bilingual ordinance prohibiting the expenditure of public funds on the use of languages other than English. Fire safety information pamphlets in Spanish are prohibited; Spanish marriage ceremonies are halted; and public transportation signs in Spanish are removed.

1981

• Sen. S. I. Hayakawa (R-CA) introduces the first amendment to the U.S. Constitution declaring English the official language of the nation. The bill dies without action.
• The Virginia legislature declares English the state's official language and makes English the language of public instruction.

1982

• Sen. Alan Simpson (R-WY) introduces S 2222, the first version of the Immigration Reform and Control Act. The measure provides amnesty to illegal aliens who have resided in the U.S. for a period of time. It passes the Senate but goes nowhere in the House.

1983

• U.S. English is founded by Dr. John Tanton, an ophthamologist from Michigan, as a project of the Federation for American Immigration Reform.
• The California Committee for Ballots in English sponsors Proposition O in San Francisco calling for a return to English Only ballots in the city. The proposition passes by 63%.

1984

• New York passes sweeping education reforms, including foreign language requirements for all students. Non-native English speakers may receive foreign language credit for their native language.

• The Indiana and Kentucky state legislatures declare English their official state language; these measures are both located in sections of the law dealing with state emblems.

• The Tennessee legislature declares English the "official and legal" language of the state. The statute further requires all official documents and communications, including ballots, to be in English, and makes English the language of public instruction.

• The House passes the Immigration Reform and Control Act. The bill contains a provision to require a "minimal understanding of ordinary English" to qualify for permanent residence status under the amnesty program.

• The Senate Subcommittee on the Constitution holds hearings on Senate Joint Resolution 167, a measure introduced by Sen. Walter Huddleston (R-KY) to declare English the official language of the United States. No further action occurs on the measure.

• The Education for Economic Security Act becomes law. Funding is provided for the improvement of teaching and instruction in foreign languages.

• The reauthorization of the Bilingual Education Act creates several new programs. Developmental bilingual education programs focus on second language study, academic excellence programs identify successful bilingual programs, and an Adult English Literacy program is added. A limited amount of funding is set aside for "alternative instruction" in which a child's native language need not be utilized.

• California voters approve Proposition 38, which calls for an end to bilingual ballots in the state. The measure places California on record in opposition to the federal law mandating such ballots.

1985

• Secretary of Education William J. Bennett delivers a speech in New York City attacking bilingual education and questioning the benefits of bilingual education over other methods, including the "sink-or-swim" approach.

• In a response to the Bennett speech, the Spanish American League Against Discrimination (SALAD) coins the term "English Plus" in describing the goals and benefits of bilingual education.

1986

• English First is founded as a project of the Committee to Protect the Family. Larry Pratt, former state representative in Virginia, serves as president.

• The American Ethnic Coalition is founded by Lou Zaeske in Texas to prevent "the division of America along language or ethnic lines."

• Congress passes the Immigration Reform and Control Act. English proficiency requirements are established for permanent resident status under the amnesty program. A "sense of Congress" resolution declaring English the official language of the nation is removed.

• Proposition 63 passes in California, the first English Language Amendment passed by ballot initiative. Included in the measure is a provision allowing California residents and anyone doing business in the state to sue if the law is not properly upheld.

• The Georgia state legislature passes a non-binding resolution declaring English the state language.

1987

• 37 state legislatures consider English Only measures; 5 pass: Arkansas, Mississippi, North Carolina, North Dakota, and South Carolina.

• North Carolina mandates foreign language instruction for all students in grades K-5.

• Norman Cousins resigns from U.S. English Board of Directors upon learning that tens of thousands of people in Los Angeles are on waiting lists for English classes.

• Linda Chavez, former Reagan appointee, is hired as the new Executive Director of U.S. English. The organization expects her to assist in improving relations with the Hispanic community.

• The English Plus Information Clearinghouse is established in Washington, DC. The coalition of education, civil rights, and ethnic groups seeks to provide information on, and a positive response to, efforts to restrict language rights in the nation.

1988

• The U.S. 9th Circuit Court of Appeals declares California's Proposition 63 "primarily a symbolic statement."

• The House Subcommittee on Civil Rights and the Constitution holds hearings on the five English language amendments pending in the 100th Congress. No further action is taken on these measures.

• Congress passes an omnibus education bill with provisions affecting bilingual education, foreign language and adult ESL programs. Increased funding is available for "alternative instruction" programs under the Bilingual Education Act; the Foreign Language Assistance Act is created to improve elementary and secondary foreign language instruction; and the English Literacy Grants Programs is created to provide ESL instruction to LEP adults.

• A memo written by John Tanton surfaces during the campaign to have English declared the official language of Arizona. The memo speculates on the negative effects of continued Hispanic immigration, including "the tradition of· the *mordida* (bribe)," "low educability," and high birth-rates. Further investigations reveal funding for U.S. English comes from questionable sources. Linda Chavez and John Tanton resign from U.S. English and Walter Cronkite steps down from its Board of Directors.

• English Language Amendments pass by ballot initiative in Arizona, Colorado and Florida. Incidents of discrimination against non-English speakers are reported on the rise in those states.

1989

• New Mexico becomes the first state in the nation to declare an English Plus policy. Washington and Oregon soon follow with English Plus statutes.

• Lowell, MA approves an English Only resolution, requesting the state legislature to declare English the official language of Massachusetts.

• Despite strong opposition from U.S. English, the New York State Board of Regents raises the exit criteria from the state's bilingual education programs from the 23rd percentile to the 40th percentile.

• Almost exactly one year after passing one of the nation's

most restrictive English language amendments, Arizona mandates foreign language instruction for all students in grades 1–8,
to be fully implemented by 1999.

ONE NATION . . . INDIVISIBLE?[2]

. . . What is it that has made a society out of the hodge-podge of
nationalities, races and colors represented in the immigrant
hordes that people our nation? It is language, of course, that has
made communication among all these elements possible. It is with
a common language that we have dissolved distrust and fear. It is
with language that we have drawn up the understandings and
agreements and social contracts that make a society possible.

But while language is a necessary cause of our oneness as a
society, it is not a sufficient cause. A foreigner cannot, by speaking
faultless English, become an Englishman. Paul Theroux, a contemporary novelist and travel writer, has commented on this fact:
"Foreigners are always aliens in England. No one becomes English. It's a very tribal society. . . . No one becomes Japanese. . . .
No one becomes Nigerian. But Nigerians, Japanese and English
become Americans."

One need not speak faultless American English to become an
American. Indeed, one may continue to speak English with an
appalling foreign accent. This is true of some of my friends, but
they are seen as fully American because of the warmth and enthu-
siasm with which they enter into the life of the communities in
which they live.

Even as the American nation was coming into being, it had
become obvious that the American experience was creating a new
kind of human being. Among the first to comment on this fact
was Thomas Paine, who wrote: "If there is a country in the world
where concord, according to common calculation, would be least
expected, it is America. Made up, as it is, of people from different
nations . . . speaking different languages, and more different in
their modes of worship, it would appear that the union of such a

[2]Speech by S. I. Hayakawa, reprinted as the *English Language Amendment: One
Nation . . . Indivisible?* 6–18 '85. Copyright © 1985 by the Washington Institute for
Values in Public Policy.

people was impracticable. But by the simple operation of constructing government on the principles of society and the rights of man, every difficulty retires, and the parts are brought into cordial unison."

Hector St. Jean Crevecoeur, in *Letters from an American Farmer,* wrote in 1782: "What then is the American, this new man? . . . I could point out to you a family whose grandfather was an Englishman, whose wife was Dutch, whose son married a French woman, and whose present four sons have four wives of different nations. He is an American who, leaving behind him all his ancient prejudices and manners, receives new ones from the new mode of life he has embraced. The Americans were once scattered all over Europe; here they are incorporated into one of the finest systems of population which has ever appeared. The American ought therefore to love his country much better than that wherein he or his forebears were born. Here the rewards of his industry follow with equal steps in the progress of his labor."

Herman Melville, in *Redburn,* published in 1849, wrote, "you cannot spill a drop of American blood without spilling the blood of the whole world. . . . We are not a narrow tribe of men. No: our blood is the flood of the Amazon, made up of a thousand noble currents all pouring into one. We are not a nation, so much as a world."

Despite the exclusion of the Chinese after 1882, the idea of immigration as "a thousand noble currents all pouring into one" continued to haunt the American imagination: Israel Zangwill's play, *The Melting Pot,* opened in New York in 1908 to enthusiastic popular acclaim, and its title, as Nathan Glazer and Daniel P. Moynihan remark, "was seized upon as a concise evocation of a profoundly significant American fact." In the play, David Quixano, the Russian Jewish immigrant—a "pogrom orphan"—has escaped to New York, and he exclaims:

Here you stand, good folk, think I, when I see them at Ellis Island . . . in your fifty groups with your fifty languages and histories, and your fifty blood hatreds and rivalries, but you won't be long like that, brothers, for these are the fires of God you've come to. . . . A fig for your feuds and vendettas! German and Frenchman, Irishman and Englishman, Jews and Russians—into the Crucible with you all! God is making the American. . . .

In the past several years strong resistance to the "melting pot" idea has arisen, especially from those who claim to speak for the Hispanic peoples. Instead of a "melting pot," they say, the national ideal should be a "salad bowl," in which different elements are thrown together but not "melted," so that the original ingredients retain their distinctive character.

In addition to the increasing size of the Spanish-speaking population in our nation, two legislative actions have released this outburst of effort on behalf of the Spanish language—and Hispanic culture.

First there was the so-called "bilingual ballot" mandated in 1975 in an amendment to the Voting Rights Act, which required foreign-language ballots when voters of selected foreign-language groups reached five percent or more of any voting district. The groups chosen to be so favored were Asian-Americans (Chinese, Filipino, Japanese, Korean), American Indians, Alaskan Natives, and "peoples of Spanish heritage," that is Puerto Ricans, Cubans and Mexican-Americans.

Sensitive as Americans have been to racism, especially since the days of the Civil Rights Movement, no one seems to have noticed the profound racism expressed in the amendment that created the "bilingual ballot." Brown people, like Mexicans and Puerto Ricans, red people, like American Indians, and yellow people, like the Japanese and Chinese, are assumed not to be smart enough to learn English. No provision is made, however, for non-English-speaking French-Canadians in Maine or Vermont, nor for the Yiddish-speaking Hassidic Jews in Brooklyn, who are white and are presumed to be able to learn English without difficulty.

Voters in San Francisco encountered ballots in Spanish and Chinese for the first time in the elections of 1980, much to their surprise, since authorizing legislation had been passed by Congress with almost no debate, no roll-call vote, and no public discussion. Naturalized Americans, who had taken the trouble to learn English to become citizens were especially angry and remain so.

Furthermore there was the Lau decision of the U.S. Supreme Court, in response to a suit brought by a Chinese of San Francisco who complained that his children were not being taught English adequately in the public schools they were attending.

Justice William O. Douglas, delivering the opinion of the Court wrote:

This class suit brought by non-English-Chinese students against . . . the San Francisco Unified School District seeks relief against the unequal educational opportunities which are alleged to violate, *inter alia*, the Four-

teenth Amendment. No specific remedy is urged upon us. Teaching English to the students of Chinese ancestry who do not speak the language is
one choice. Giving instructions to this group in Chinese is another. There
may be others. Petitioners ask only that the Board of Education be directed to apply its expertise to the problem and rectify the situation.

Justice Douglas' decision, concurred in by the entire Court,
granted the Lau petition.

Because the Lau decision did not specify the method by which
English was to be taught, it turned out to be a go-ahead for
amazing educational developments, not so much for the Chinese
as for Hispanics, who appropriated the decision and took it to
apply especially to themselves.

The New Department of Education, established during the
Carter administration, was eager to make its presence known by
expanding its bureaucracy and its influence. The Department
quickly announced a vast program with federal funding for bilingual education, which led to the hiring of Spanish-speaking
teachers by the thousands.

The Department furthermore issued what were known as the
"Lau regulations," which required under threat of withdrawal of
federal funds that (1) non-English-speaking pupils be taught English, and that (2) academic subjects be taught in the pupils' own
language. The contradiction between these two regulations seems
not to have occurred to the educational theorists in the Department of Education. Nor does it seem to trouble, to this day, the
huge membership of the National Association for Bilingual Education.

"Bilingual education," rapidly became a growth industry, requiring more and more teachers. Complaints began to arise from
citizens that "bilingual education" was not bilingual at all, since
many Spanish-speaking teachers hired for the program were
found not to be able to speak English. But the Department of
Education decreed that teachers in the "bilingual" program do
not need to know English!

Despite the ministrations of the Department of Education, or
perhaps because of them, Hispanic students to a shocking degree,
drop out of school, educated neither in Hispanic nor in American
language and culture.

"Hispanics are the least educated minority in America, according to a report by the American Council on Education,"
writes Earl Byrd in *The Washington Times* (July 3, 1984).

"The report says 50 percent of all Hispanic youths in America drop out of high school, and only 7 percent finish college. Twelve percent of black youths and 23 percent of whites finish college."

"Eighteen percent of all Hispanics in America who are 25 or older are classified as functional illiterates, compared to 10 percent for blacks and 3 percent for whites."

I welcome the Hispanic—and as a Californian, I welcome especially the Mexican—influence on our culture. My wife was wise enough to insist that both our son and daughter learn Spanish as children and to keep reading Spanish as they were growing up. Consequently, my son, a newspaper man, was able to work for six months as an exchange writer for a newspaper in Costa Rica, while a Costa Rican reporter took my son's place in Oregon. My daughter, a graduate of the University of California at Santa Cruz, speaks Spanish, French, and after a year in Monterey Language School, Japanese.

The ethnic chauvinism of the present Hispanic leadership is an unhealthy trend in present-day America. It threatens a division perhaps more ominous in the long run than the division between blacks and whites. Blacks and whites have problems enough with each other, to be sure, but they quarrel with each other in one language. Even Malcolm X, in his fiery denunciations of the racial situation in America, wrote excellent and eloquent English.

But the present politically ambitious "Hispanic Caucus" looks forward to a destiny for Spanish-speaking Americans separate from that of Anglo-, Italian-, Polish-, Greek-, Lebanese-, Chinese-, Afro-Americans and all the rest of us who rejoice in our ethnic diversity, which give us our richness as a culture, and the English language, which keeps us in communication with each other to create a unique and vibrant culture.

The advocates of Spanish language and Hispanic culture are not at all unhappy about the fact that "bilingual education," originally instituted as the best way to teach English, often results in no English being taught at all. Nor does Hispanic leadership seem to be alarmed that large populations of Mexican-Americans, Cubans, and Puerto Ricans do not speak English and have no intention of learning.

Hispanic spokesmen rejoice when still another concession is made to the Spanish-speaking public, such as the Spanish-language "Yellow Pages" telephone directory now available in Los Angeles.

"Let's face it. We are not going to be a totally English-speaking country any more," says Aurora Helton of the Governor of Oklahoma's" Hispanic Advisory Committee.

"Spanish should be included in commercials shown throughout America. Every American child ought to be taught both English and Spanish," says Mario Obledo, president of the League of United Latin American Citizens (LULAC), which was founded more than a half-century ago to help Hispanics learn English and enter the American mainstream.

"Citizenship is what makes us all American. Language is not necessary to the system. Nowhere does the Constitution say that English is our language," says Maurice Ferre, Mayor of Miami, Florida.

"Nowhere does the Constitution say that English is our language," says Mayor Ferre.

It was to correct this omission that I introduced in April 1981 a constitutional amendment which read as follows:

"Article—

Section 1. The English language shall be the official language of the United States. . . .

Section 2. The Congress shall have the power to enforce this article by appropriate legislation."

But the movement to make English the official language of the nation is clearly gaining momentum. It is likely to suffer an occasional setback in state legislatures because of the doctrinaire liberals' assumption that every demand made by an ethnic minority must be yielded to. But whenever the question of English as the official language has been submitted to a popular referendum or ballot initiative, it has won by a majority of 70% or better.

It is not without significance that pressure against English language legislation does not come from any immigrant group other than the Hispanic: not from the Chinese or Koreans or Filipinos or Vietnamese, nor from immigrant Iranians, Turks, Greeks, East Indians, Ghananians, Ethiopians, Italians or Swedes. The only people who have any quarrel with the English language are the Hispanics—at least the Hispanic politicians and "bilingual" teachers and lobbying organizations.

One wonders about the Hispanic rank-and-file. Are they all in agreement with their leadership?

And what does it profit the Hispanic leadership if it gains power and fame, while 50% of the boys and girls of their communities, speaking little or no English, cannot make it through high school?

For the first time in our history, our nation is faced with the possibility of the kind of linguistic division that has torn apart Canada in recent years; that has been a major feature of the unhappy history of Belgium, split into speakers of French and Flemish; that is at this very moment a bloody division between the Sinhalese and Tamil populations of Sri Lanka.

None of these divisions is simply a quarrel about language. But in each case political differences become hardened and made immeasurably more difficult to resolve when they are accompanied by differences of language—and therefore conflicts of ethnic pride.

The aggressive movement on the part of Hispanics to reject assimilation and to seek to maintain—and give official status to— a foreign language within our borders is an unhealthy development. This foreign language and culture are to be maintained not through private endeavors such as those of the Alliance Francaise, which tries to preserve French language and culture, but by federal and state legislation and funding.

The energetic lobbying of the National Association for Bilingual Education and the congressional Hispanic Caucus has led to sizeable allocations for bilingual education in the Department of Education; $142 million in fiscal 1985, of which the lion's share goes to Hispanic programs. The purpose of this allocation at the federal level is to prepare administrators and teachers for bilingual education at the state level—which means additional large sums of money allocated for this purpose by state governments.

In brief, the basic directive of the Lau decision of the Supreme Court has been, for all intents and purposes, diverted from its original purpose of teaching English. . . .

One official language and one only, so that we can unite as a nation. This is what President Theodore Roosevelt also perceived when he said:

We have room for but one language here, and that is the English language, for we intend to see that the crucible turns our people out as Americans. . . . No more hyphenated Americans.

Let me quote in conclusion a remark from the distinguished American novelist, Saul Bellow, when he agreed to serve on the advisory board of our national organization, U.S. English:

Melting pot, yes. Tower of Babel, no!

TOWARDS A UNITED AMERICA[3]

The tie of language is perhaps the strongest and the most durable that can unite mankind.

Alexis de Tocqueville, 1805–1859

U.S. English is the leading national citizens' action group dedicated to preserving the unifying role of a common language in America. While multilingual people may be an asset to a nation, a government of many languages is a formula for divisiveness and disaster. In trying to guarantee equal official status to competing languages, chaos reigns in the states of the former Soviet Union and Yugoslavia, and in such nations as Canada, Belgium, Sri Lanka, India and Afghanistan. U.S. English is alarmed by the potential for divisiveness in our own country.

Did you know that:
• The U.S. Government has not adopted English as our official language?
• More than 75% of Americans want English as our official language?
• 69 nations have designated one official language for government business?
• Hundreds of thousands of children in this country are being educated primarily in languages other than English?
• Students are allowed to graduate from high school without learning English?
• Four states—Washington, Oregon, Rhode Island and New Mexico—have taken official action in support of multilingualism in government?
• Drivers' license tests are now given in over a dozen different languages?
• We are spending billions of taxpayers' dollars on multilingual governmental and educational programs?

Making English the official language in the United States is crucial to our ability to communicate with each other and to maintain our national unity.

The mission of U.S. English is to preserve our common bond

[3]Brochure from U.S. English 1993. Copyright © 1993 by U.S. English. Reprinted with permission.

by making English the official language of government in the United States and by promoting opportunities for people living here to learn English.

The objectives of U.S. English are to promote:
- Passage of legislation at the national, state and local levels to declare English as our official language;
- Action to end policies which require government agencies to conduct their official business in multiple languages;
- Enforcement of the English language and civics requirements for naturalization;
- English proficiency as a national priority; and,
- Expanded opportunities to learn English quickly in our schools and in the workplace.

Americans are remarkably diverse in national origin, race, language, ethnicity, religion and culture. A common language is crucial to our ability to understand each other and to maintain our national unity.

Founded in 1983, U.S. English is confident in its accomplishments and looks forward with renewed dedication to making English the foundation for a strong, united America.

Past and ongoing activities include:

In Washington: Over the last four years, more than a third of the members of the U.S. House of Representatives have joined in sponsorship of elements of the "Language for All Peoples Initiative," consisting of legislation to make English the official language of government, the extension of income tax credits to employers to help cover the cost of English language education programs for employees who have limited English proficiency and a "sense of Congress" resolution setting forth objectives for a common language policy for our nation. Support for companion legislation in the U.S. Senate continues to grow.

In The States: Since U.S. English was founded, fourteen states have passed laws declaring English their official language, including California, Arizona, Colorado, and Florida. Nineteen states now have English as their official language. In states where referenda have been held, more than 10 million Americans have voted to make English our common language. U.S. English has led the way in all these states. Each year, U.S. English targets more states and assists voters in their efforts to make English the official language of their home states.

In The Courts: U.S. English has won a number of lawsuits in the federal and state courts in language-related cases, successfully defending the position of the legality and benefits of having English as our official, common language. Several cases are now pending.

In The Media: Using print ads in newspapers and magazines, television and radio appearances, and through contacts with magazines and newspapers, U.S. English has made millions of Americans aware of the value of our common language and the importance of efforts to preserve it.

In Education: U.S. English has worked directly with teachers to improve language instruction for children and adults. U.S. English has testified before legislative hearings in favor of educational improvement, parental choice and program accountability on the local, state and federal levels. U.S. English has also developed a series of adult literacy programs for use at home and in the workplace.

ENGLISH PLUS: STATEMENT OF PURPOSE[4]

The core of the strength and vitality of the United States is the diversity of our people, and our constitutional commitment to equal protection under the law. Now, more than ever, our commitment to cultural and democratic pluralism is essential to enhance our competitiveness and position of international leadership. In an interdependent world, the diversity of our people provides a unique reservoir of understanding and talent.

In order to sustain and strengthen these values and the national interest, the undersigned organizations have come together to address more effectively the role of language in the national and international community. We have agreed to a statement of principles and objectives, and to establish EPIC, the English Plus Information Clearinghouse.

The English Plus concept holds that the national interest can best be served when all members of our society have full access to effective opportunities to acquire strong English language profi-

    [4]Unsigned article. From *Epic Events* 2(4): 2 '89. Copyright © 1989 by National Immigration, Refugee and Citizenship Forum. Reprinted with permission.

ciency *plus* mastery of a second or multiple languages. English Plus holds that there is a need for a vastly extended network of facilities and programs for comprehensive instruction in English and other languages.

English Plus rejects the ideology and divisive character of the so-called English Only movement. English Plus holds that national unity and our constitutional values require that language assistance be made available in order to ensure equal access to essential services, education, the electoral process and other rights and opportunities guaranteed to all members of society.

The undersigned organizations have agreed to establish a national clearinghouse to facilitate the exchange of information in order to strengthen programs and advocacy consistent with our shared values, common objectives and the national interest.

In establishing EPIC, the founding member organizations have agreed to the following resolution:

WHEREAS English is and will remain the primary language of the United States, and all members of our society recognize the importance of English to national life, individual accomplishment, and personal enrichment; and

WHEREAS many U.S. citizens have native languages other than English, including many languages indigenous to this continent, and many members of our society have not had an equal opportunity to learn English; and

WHEREAS the ability to communicate in English and other languages has promoted and can further enhance American economic, political and cultural vitality; and contributes to our nation's productivity, worldwide competitiveness, successful international diplomacy and national security; and

WHEREAS English Only and other restrictionist language legislation has the potential for abridging the citizen's right to vote, eroding other civil rights, fostering governmental interference in private activity and free commerce, and causing social disunity; and

WHEREAS the organizations establishing the English Plus Information Clearinghouse are committed to the principles of democratic and cultural pluralism and encourage respect for the cultural and linguistic heritages of all members of our society;

BE IT THEREFORE RESOLVED:

1. There is a need for a vastly extended network of facilities for comprehensive English language instruction and services to ensure all persons the ability to exercise the rights and responsibilities of full participation in society.

2. There is a need to foster multiple language skills among all of our people in order to promote our position in the world marketplace and to strengthen the conduct of foreign relations.

3. There is a need to encourage the retention and development of a person's first language, to build upon the multiple language skills of all members of our society, and to strengthen our commitment to cultural and democratic pluralism.

4. There is a need to retain and strengthen the full range of language assistance policies and programs, including bilingual assistance, to ensure all members of society an equal opportunity to exercise their rights and responsibilities in the electoral process, education, the legal system, social services and health care.

5. There is a need to reject the objectives and premises of English Only and promote the concept of English Plus to promote public civility and the fundamental values and objectives of our society.

6. There is a need to defeat any legislative initiative on the federal, state or local level which would mandate English as the official language and thereby restrict the civil rights, civil liberties or equal opportunities of all persons, including persons with limited English proficiency.

7. There is a need for an English Plus Information Clearinghouse to facilitate and enhance: the exchange of information, public education, advocacy, effective policies and programs, and cooperation among a wide range of communities, private organizations and public sector entities.

8. The National Forum and the Joint National Committee for Languages will provide the auspices for the staff and information activities of the English Plus Information Clearinghouse.

PRO-CON: SHOULD ENGLISH BE OUR OFFICIAL LANGUAGE[5]

Quick, what's the official language of the United States? English, right? Wrong. Although most Americans speak English, U.S. lawmakers have never proclaimed an official national language. Now, however, the rising tide of immigrants is making some Americans wonder if they should.

In order to accommodate the growing number of Americans who do not speak English, many schools, businesses, and government agencies now offer their services in a variety of languages. But some citizens see the trend toward a multilingual society as dangerous. They believe it will fragment the country into dozens of hostile ethnic enclaves.

The debate has crystallized around a proposal that would make English the official language of the U.S. government. Although the law would allow for private use of any language, public documents, such as voting ballots, and government programs, such as schools, could only use English. Already 14 states have passed laws making English their official language, most of them within the past two years. On one side of the controversy, groups such as U.S. English lobby for "official-English" laws nationwide. On the other side, civil liberty groups and ethnic organizations argue that such laws are motivated by fear of America's immigrants. Should Congress pass a law making English our official national language?

Pro: Immigrants to the United States should be strongly encouraged to master the English language. Otherwise, they will never be able to gain a good education, find a fulfilling job, or fully participate in our democratic society. But government programs such as bilingual public education, multilingual voting ballots, and foreign-language driver's license exams only foster a

---

[5]From *Scholastic Update*, May 6, 1988. Copyright © 1988 by Scholastic Inc. Reprinted by permission of the publisher.

divided society. New immigrants can coast by on their native tongue without ever having to learn English.

Countries that support bilingualism, such as Canada, become violently divided into language-group factions. To avoid such a fate, we must insist that English—our common bond—be our nation's only official language.

Con: A law making English the official U.S. language wouldn't lead to a more harmonious society. It would merely promote xenophobia, the fear of immigrants and their culture. Such a law would deprive Americans who do not speak English of their basic rights.

For instance, if ballots were only printed in English, Spanish-speaking American citizens would be denied their right to vote. If an Asian-American with little command of English was hit by a car, how could she receive medical treatment from doctors legally compelled to speak only English?

Because English is obviously the path to success in this country, there is already ample incentive for new immigrants to learn English. In fact, so many new arrivals want to learn the language that schools in Los Angeles report 40,000 people on waiting lists for night courses.

Our country can be enriched by a variety of languages. In face, we should encourage everyone to learn more languages, not fewer. It would strengthen our competitive edge in trade, improve foreign relations, and enhance communication in our diverse society.

II. HISTORICAL, POLITICAL, AND LEGAL IMPACTS

EDITOR'S INTRODUCTION

Studying history helps one to understand better the cause behind events in the present day. This section describes language debates at various points in American history, relates how several different states resolved the political debate, and cites recent legal rulings on language laws.

The first article in this section, Language Politics and American Identity" by Jack Citrin, points out that the struggle for Americans to achieve both political unity and cultural diversity is as old as the nation itself. He argues that the official English movement is often misperceived as fueled only by prejudice, but the activating sentiment among its supporters appears to be patriotism rather than intolerance. The author concludes by presenting his own framework for language policy.

James C. Stalker, a professor at Michigan State University, is the author of the next article, reprinted from the *English Journal.* By providing a history of some language debates and decisions, he attempts to clarify the issues and presents an argument for English as the nation's common language, but not necessarily as the official or only language. Stalker argues that economic and politic advantage is a more powerful incentive for a person to learn English than any legislation could ever be.

Writing in the *American School Board Journal,* James Crawford, a journalist and author of several publications on bilingual education, disposes of what he considers to be misconceptions used by advocates of official English. He notes that the official-English movement has the potential to threaten bilingual services for limited-English speakers and to further ethnic stereotypes and prejudices. Crawford presents the four most common arguments in favor of the official English amendment and attempts to refute each.

The fourth article, from *CQ Researcher,* recounts the language issue as it played out in Dade County, Florida, in the early 1980s and again in 1993. An urban area with one of the largest Hispanic populations in the country, Dade County often serves as a barometer for attitudes towards minorities and bilingualism.

Next, an article from the *Arizona English Bulletin* discusses the issues and political images used in a 1988 Arizona campaign to pass an official language amendment. The amendment was passed, and Karen L. Adams, a professor at Arizona State University, points out that often the same images, such as an American flag, were used by both proponents and opponents in the debate. Then, Roberto Rodriquez, writing in *Hispanic*, describes the 1990 district court ruling that struck down the very same amendment on the basis that it violated the right of free speech guaranteed by the First Amendment. The court's decision, on a case brought by a state employee who claimed she was prohibited from speaking Spanish in the course of her job, nullified what has been described as one of the most restrictive official language laws in the nation.

A more recent court case, decided in late 1993, is the subject of Harriet Chiang's article from the *San Francisco Chronicle*. In this decision, the California Supreme Court ruled that over-the-counter drugs do not have to include warning labels in a language other than English. The case was watched closely by Hispanic groups because the drug manufacturer had advertised the product heavily on Spanish-speaking television.

LANGUAGE POLITICS AND AMERICAN IDENTITY[1]

In recent years, America's ability to reconcile political unity and cultural diversity has been challenged anew. A massive wave of immigration from Latin America and Asia has transformed the character of many local communities and fueled demands for bilingual government services. The specter of linguistic diversity, in turn, has sparked insecurity about national cohesion and fostered a movement to designate English as the official language of the United States.

Underlying the political confrontation between "language

[1]Article by Jack Citrin. From *The Public Interest* Spring 1990. Copyright © 1990 by National Affairs Inc. Reprinted by permission.

rights" and "English only" is a deeper debate over the meaning of American identity and the means of preserving it. Is speaking English a condition of full membership in American society? Does government support for bilingualism erode the foundations of national unity, or does it enhance ethnic harmony?

Policymakers and voters have been answering these questions in different ways. Even as a stream of federal laws, court decisions, and administrative regulations has favored the use of other languages in public institutions, most citizens regard English as a symbol of American nationhood that must be defended. A language policy that ignores this entrenched public view is bound to be resisted. But is there any policy that could simultaneously promote a common civic identity, ethnic tolerance, and equal economic opportunity?

Linguistic Conflict in America

Although the Framers of the Constitution ultimately decided not to endow English with a special legal status, they assumed that a common language would develop in the United States and that it would be English. True to this assumption, researchers consistently find that the typical pattern of language usage among immigrants to America is a rapid shift from non-English monolingualism in the first generation to bilingualism in the second generation, and then to English monolingualism in the third generation. During most of the nineteenth century, this shift occurred not because of governmental coercion but in spite of laws that were relatively favorable to the maintenance of one's mother tongue. Immigrants and their descendants quickly learned English—not because they were forced to, but because learning English helped them to get ahead in America.

Nevertheless, an "English only" strain in public opinion did develop around the turn of the century, as a wave of immigration from southern and eastern Europe stirred up xenophobic feelings. A little later, the strong anti-German sentiment engendered by World War I stimulated new claims that the stability of American institutions and values depended on cultural homogeneity. The Americanization movement that flourished at this time emphasized the need for a common language to speed the assimilation of immigrants with alien traditions, and fifteen states passed laws making English the only language of instruction in the schools. In 1924 Congress also acted to assuage nativist anxieties by establishing immigration quotas overwhelmingly favorable to applicants from northwestern Europe. Language issues then vanished from the national agenda for almost fifty years.

The interplay of the political and demographic changes that began in the 1960s ushered in a new era of conflict over language. First blacks and then other groups increasingly emphasized the values of ethnic solidarity and distinctiveness. A political climate emerged in which policies came to be judged according to their perceived potential for strengthening or weakening a group's ethnic heritage. In this context, Hispanic activists articulated the concept of language rights as a constitutional entitlement that deserved "equal protection of the laws." Specifically, they called on government to go beyond the mere toleration of minority languages in the private sphere to the active promotion of bilingualism in public institutions.

Official actions designed to support linguistic minorities wishing to maintain their native cultures precipitated the organized drive to endow English with a special legal status. Bilingual-education programs were the main catalyst. The 1968 Bilingual Education Act was the first significant federal step in the promotion of language rights. This measure provided funds to meet "the special educational needs . . . of children of limited English-speaking ability," defined as "children who come from environments where the dominant language is other than English." Senator Ralph Yarborough, the sponsor of the bill, declared that his intention was "just to try to make those children fully literate in English," but it is clear that for many Hispanic leaders and activists bilingual education represented a vehicle for resisting cultural assimilation and encouraging the continued use of Spanish.

Implementation of the Bilingual Education Act became a hotly contested issue. Minority activists tended to favor cultural-maintenance programs that teach children most subjects in both their native language and English throughout their educations. This approach repudiates the melting pot in favor of a "multicultural" conception of American identity that celebrates ethnic consciousness. The symbolic importance of this diminished respect for English is the likely reason for the overwhelming public rejection of the bicultural approach, reported in a 1983 national survey conducted by UCLA political scientists David Sears and Leonie Huddy. The survey found that the majority "Anglo" group accepts bilingual-education programs that stress the rapid acquisition of English proficiency.

Despite this popular opinion, court decisions and administrative decrees tended to favor bicultural or lengthy "transitional" programs. In *Lau v. Nichols* (1974), the Supreme Court decided that Title VI of the 1964 Civil Rights Act required school districts to take steps to ensure that non-English-speaking children can participate meaningfully in the educational system; while the Court did not specify what steps should be taken, the so-called *Lau* guidelines proposed by the Department of Health, Education and Welfare's Office of Civil Rights were heavily weighted against English-as-a-Second-Language programs.

These regulations were bitterly opposed, particularly by influential teachers' unions, and in 1978 the pendulum at both the federal and state levels began to swing away from official promotion of bilingualism. A four-year evaluation of bilingual-education programs conducted by the American Institutes for Research and released in 1977–1978 played a crucial role. This study found no convincing evidence showing that bilingual-education programs were effective in improving English proficiency or in increasing academic motivation. There was evidence, however, that such programs resulted in the classroom segregation of Hispanic children. In response, Congress became increasingly receptive to efforts to broaden the range of programs funded under the Bilingual Education Act to include structured-immersion programs, which "immerse" students in English-speaking classrooms. With the advent of the Reagan administration, skepticism about native-language instruction dominated official thinking; the advocates of language rights, along with other members of the civil-rights coalition, were placed on the defensive.

Together with domestic political trends, changing patterns of immigration prepared the ground for the spread of an "official English" movement. In 1965 immigration legislation abolished both the national-origins system and the explicit exclusion of Asians. The new law also raised the ceiling on the number of immigrants and gave priority in the allocation of immigration visas to applicants with family members already in the United States.

The results were a huge increase in the number of legal immigrants and a marked shift in their racial and linguistic backgrounds. Immigration and Naturalization Service figures show that between 1950 and 1960 roughly 2.5 million people legally emigrated to the United States; there were 570,000 legal immigrants in 1985 alone. Between 1921 and 1960, 18 percent of America's legal immigrants came from Latin America and only 4 percent came from Asia. Between 1971 and 1980, by contrast, the corresponding figures were 40 percent and 35 percent, while in the next five years 35 percent came from Latin America and 48 percent came from Asia. There also was a large inflow of Spanish-speaking illegal immigrants, principally from Mexico.

Along with the sheer number of immigrants, their geographic concentration—the Asians in metropolitan areas in California, the Hispanics in states close to the Mexican border—increased the visibility of foreign customs and values. To some, it also raised the possibility of a territorial basis for linguistic separatism.

The Call For "Official English"

Language rights were demanded by ethnic minorities as a symbolic affirmation of their continuing attachment to their original cultures. In the context of increasing immigration and growing anxiety about America's prestige and power in the international arena, however, the revival of ethnic consciousness aroused concern about national unity. In 1983, warning that the failure to maintain a common language in the United States would produce the unrest and polarization experienced by Canada, Belgium, and other linguistically divided countries, Senator S. I. Hayakawa and a Michigan ophthalmologist named John Tanton founded the organization U.S. English to ensure the preservation of English as America's national language.

One of U.S. English's early goals was a constitutional amendment to declare English the official language. Senator Hayakawa first proposed such a measure in 1981; his English Language Amendment (ELA) also would have given Congress the power to enforce the official status of English with appropriate legislation. Other members of Congress periodically have reintroduced the ELA, but the measure has made no substantial legislative progress.

With the failure of the ELA in Congress, U.S. English has turned its attention to the state and local levels. Due largely to the efforts of U.S. English and its sympathizers, forty-four states and numerous counties and municipalities have considered "official English" laws or initiatives since 1981. Before 1980, only three states—Nebraska, Illinois, and Virginia—had declared English their sole "official" language. Today only three states—Maine,

Vermont, and Alaska—have yet to consider "official English" laws. The legislatures of Arkansas, Georgia, Indiana, Kentucky, Mississippi, North Carolina, North Dakota, South Carolina, and Tennessee adopted such measures, and Virginia amended its earlier declaration to discourage bilingual education. In thirty-four states, however, the legislatures refused to pass "official English" statutes. In four of these states—California, Arizona, Colorado, and Florida—English-language amendments to the state constitutions were subsequently placed on the ballot through the initiative process and adopted by popular vote.

In many states, support for "official English" took the form of a simple declarative resolution. A few states, such as South Carolina and Tennessee, went further and prohibited the use of foreign languages in specified public institutions such as schools and the courts. The implementation of these provisions was left to legislators, administrators, and judges, and it is generally agreed that the impact of state "official English" laws has been almost entirely symbolic. But whatever the local differences in the content of "official English" measures, the deeply emotional debates that they engender have a remarkable consistency.

Proponents of the measures contend that both historical experience and common sense teach that linguistic diversity threatens political cohesion and stability. Previous generations of immigrants understood that learning English was the vehicle of social integration and economic mobility. For English to lose its status as America's common tongue is, therefore, to risk a Tower of Babel and to undermine one of the last things that still binds this pluralistic society together.

Proponents deny that they are hostile to minorities; indeed, many of the movement's leading spokesmen have immigrant origins. Adoption of their proposals, they claim, would not eliminate bilingual programs that genuinely advance the process of acculturation, but only check the development of policies that threaten to erode a common sense of American identity and to prevent immigrants from moving out of economically depressed linguistic enclaves.

Opponents of "official English" measures portray them as instruments of exclusion rather than assimilation. To enshrine the superior status of English in the Constitution, they claim, is to state that linguistic minorities are inferior and unwanted in America. They argue further that the predominance of English usage is not in danger; they cite studies showing that virtually all immigrants want to learn English and do so, despite the inadequate supply of English instruction for adults. To its critics, then, the campaign for "official English" is at best unnecessary and at worst a thinly veiled form of racism and xenophobia. Whatever the manifest content of proposed English-language amendments to state constitutions, opponents contend that such proposals augur future discrimination against language minorities. In their view, "official English" measures both endanger bilingual services and run counter to America's historical commitment to tolerance and equality.

One might expect proposals for "official English" to be most likely to succeed in states with large concentrations of Hispanics or Asians, because the visible clash of ethnic strains might generate resentment among English-speaking groups. In fact, if one considers only outcomes in state legislatures, the opposite seems true. State "official English" laws are concentrated mainly in southern states with largely Anglo-Saxon populations and tiny proportions of foreign-born, Hispanic, or Asian residents. Under these conditions, language usage is a settled matter, bilingualism a remote issue, and the designation of English as the state's official language an uncontroversial decision. On the other hand, in states with substantial language minorities, the legislatures have defeated or tabled "official English" proposals. In these states, politically active members of ethnic groups have persuaded politicians in both parties to resist attacks on bilingual programs.

The reluctance of elected officials to act, however, does not always seal the fate of "official English." Significantly, the four states in which voters have overridden their legislators to pass English-language amendments to their state constitutions have, as a group, the highest proportions of non-English speakers, immigrants, Hispanics, and Asians.

At the local or regional level, then, English becomes a salient and highly emotional issue when rapid immigration changes the prevailing pattern of language usage. In this context, leaders of both major political parties have chosen to avoid disturbing the existing language policy. But where supporters of "official English" have been sufficiently well organized to put the issue to a popular vote, they have carried the day by wide margins.

Voting on "Official English"

In November 1986, California voters endorsed Proposition 63, an English-language amendment to the state's constitution.

The stated purpose of this initiative, which was the model for the initiatives passed two years later in Arizona, Colorado, and Florida, was to "preserve, protect and strengthen the English language, the common language of the people of the United States." The initiative also instructed the state's legislature to enforce the status of English as the official language of California and to make no law that "diminishes or ignores" the role of English. Residents and people doing business in California were to have legal standing to sue the state to ensure enforcement of the amendment.

With the single exception of Republican Senator Pete Wilson, all of the state's leading politicians opposed Proposition 63. Governor Deukmejian called it "unnecessary" and warned that "it would cause fear, confusion and resentment among many minority Californians." The state's Roman Catholic bishops also urged the defeat of the "official English" initiative, stating that it would "enshrine prejudice in the law and jeopardize all forms of bilingual assistance." The state attorney general agreed, calling Proposition 63 "an open invitation to hundreds of hurtful and frivolous lawsuits," while the Los Angeles City Council deemed the proposal "contrary to our most basic principles of equality and opportunity" and asserted that it would "result in a sense of inferiority, debasement and shame in one's own ethnic heritage."

An impressive coalition of interest groups, including the League of Women Voters, local chambers of commerce, the state AFL-CIO, the ACLU, and organizations of ethnic minorities echoed these charges, as did editorials in the state's largest newspapers. On election day, however, 73 percent of the electorate statewide, and a majority in every single county, opted for "official English." An exit poll conducted by the Field Institute indicated widespread support for the amendment in almost every segment of the California electorate. To be sure, Hispanic and Asian voters were less likely to approve the amendment than were black or white voters, but support did not differ significantly between blacks and whites. The young and highly educated were relatively less likely to vote for "official English" than the rest of the public, but even among these groups—including respondents with postgraduate degrees—majorities reported having supported the amendment. Economic concerns did not appear to influence voting; there was no difference in the level of support for Proposition 63 between people who said that they were better off financially than they were a year ago and people who said that their circumstances had worsened.

The cracks in the general consensus about the desirability of "official English" were related to party and ideology. Eighty-four percent of the Republicans surveyed favored the amendment, compared with 56 percent of the Democrats. This divergence in outlook grows even larger when voters are compared according to ideological identification: conservatives were much more likely than liberals to support the proposition. It appears that differences of opinion on language issues result more from differences in attitudes toward social issues than from economic cleavages.

The 1988 campaigns for "official English" in Arizona, Colorado, and Florida closely resembled the 1986 campaign in California. Once again, the top elected officials in both political parties; prominent figures in education, religion, and the judicial system; important business and labor organizations; minority-group leaders; and the leading newspapers opposed the measures as unnecessary, divisive, racist, and destructive of necessary bilingual services. And once again, the voters opted for the amendment. The Florida amendment received 84 percent of the statewide vote, won in every county, and carried nearly two-thirds of the vote in heavily Hispanic Dade County. Colorado's version of "official English" passed by a three-to-two ratio. In Arizona, however, a more restrictive version of "official English" was adopted as an amendment to the state's constitution by the narrowest of margins, 51 percent to 49 percent. (In February 1990, however, a federal district judge in Phoenix ruled that the amendment was an unconstitutional violation of the federally guaranteed right of free speech. Whether this decision will be appealed and how it ultimately will affect other state and local "official English" laws remain to be seen. In any case, the court's action stands as another example of the gap between public officials and popular sentiment.)

A pre-election poll of Arizona voters conducted by the *Arizona Republic* indicated that Republicans (67 percent), respondents without any college education (66 percent), and those over fifty-five years old (64 percent) were more likely to support the English-language amendment than Democrats (47 percent), college graduates (44 percent), and people aged eighteen to thirty-four (56 percent). In Florida, however, a survey conducted by Mason-Dixon Opinion Research found no differences in support for "official English" among self-identified Republicans, Democrats, and independents, doubtless a reflection of the greater conservatism of Florida Democrats as compared with those in

California or Arizona. As in California, in Florida both whites (79 percent) and blacks (75 percent) strongly supported the amendment, but Hispanics (25 percent) were strongly opposed.

These data, however sparse, make it clear why proposals for "official English" have a good chance of succeeding at the polls. Even large Hispanic or Asian communities often have little electoral power, because these groups tend to include many noncitizens and to have low levels of political participation. The political right is the core of the "official English" movement, but the movement attracts support from all along the ideological spectrum. Despite the condemnation of party leaders, civil-rights organizations, and the intelligentsia, a majority of Democratic and black voters, apparently unaware of or unpersuaded by claims that these measures are grounded in prejudice and xenophobia, have approved English-language amendments.

Language and American Identity

Economic competition and cultural resentment are social science's leading explanations for linguistic conflict. These causal theories may differ in their predictions concerning the specific groups that are likely to support "official English" and to oppose bilingualism. But both theories characterize the desire to elevate the status of English as a hostile, defensive reaction to feelings of vulnerability, based variously on ethnic competition for jobs, education, or housing; resentment about the cost of public services that primarily benefit linguistic minorities; unfavorable personal experiences with members of these groups; insecurity about the loss of American power; or sheer prejudice.

No doubt there are voters whose positions on language issues are determined by such motives. The support for "official English" is so pervasive, however, that economic anxiety and prejudice against minorities can hardly be its only or even its primary causes. Indeed, most of the respondents in a 1987 California poll, conducted after the passage of the state's English-language amendment, declared that it was a "good thing" for immigrants to preserve their native languages and customs. A February 1988 California poll found that only 18 percent of the Anglo respondents were "very worried" that the increased number of Hispanics and Asians in the state would make it hard to maintain the "American way of life"; only 13 percent reported that this change had harmed them or their families. In a June 1986 CBS

News/*New York Times* national survey, 68 percent of the respondents said that they would welcome "today's new immigrants" into their neighborhoods, and only 15 percent were worried that these immigrants would take away their jobs. In sum, most people do not appear very anxious about the personal economic impact of immigration, nor is there pervasive animosity toward linguistic minorities and their cultures.

The polls suggest an alternative explanation for the public's prevailing outlook on language policy: the popular conception of national-identity equates being American with speaking English. Thus the February 1988 California poll found that 76 percent of those surveyed, including 65 percent of those with a college degree and more than two-thirds of the Hispanic and Asian respondents, believed that "speaking and writing English" are "very important" in making someone a "true American." Although a conservative political outlook predictably boosted support for this normative conception of American nationality, perhaps the strongest indication of the positive symbolism associated with "official English" is that fully 62 percent of the respondents who identified themselves as strong liberals and 65 percent of those who called themselves strong Democrats also endorsed it.

What is more, although 75 percent of this sample felt that voting in elections was another very important criterion in defining a "true American," 62 percent said that only citizens who can speak and read English should be allowed to vote. In a 1986 Roper national survey, 81 percent of the sample agreed that "anyone who wants to stay in this country should have to learn English." And a November 1986 CBS News/*New York Times* national poll found that two-thirds of those surveyed thought that English already was the official language of the United States. In this climate, a vote for "official English" can be taken as an expression—sometimes self-conscious, sometimes reflexive—of one's identification with an important symbol of nationality.

A major reason for the success of "official English" at the polls is that its advocates have succeeded in defining the measure as a show of patriotism rather than intolerance. When asked why they intended to vote for the English-language amendment, 59 percent of the registered California voters polled just before the 1986 election said that they simply believed that "if you live in the United States you should be able to speak English."

Along with Donald Green, Beth Reingold, and Evelyn Walters, I conducted an elaborate statistical analysis of California opinion on language issues. We concluded that neither a person's immediate economic circumstances nor the perceived *personal* impacts of ethnic change were significant indicators of attitudes toward bilingualism. To be sure, there are groups—linguistic minorities themselves, schoolteachers forced to implement bilingual-education programs, residents of communities where the influx of immigrants has unsettled the established fabric of daily life—directly affected by language policy. But for most members of the dominant language group, the short-term personal consequences are quite limited. Under these circumstances, underlying political orientations—such as social conservatism or egalitarianism—are the primary determinants of policy preferences.

The intertwined debates over "official English" and bilingualism reflect a cultural conflict over the meaning of American identity. A large segment of the public believes that becoming an American means speaking English; for these people, learning English figures prominently in the process whereby successive waves of immigrants become full-fledged citizens by their own efforts at assimilation. "Official English," to many, is a code word for a common nationality; hence it wins support all along the political spectrum. By challenging the special status of English, bilingualism becomes a symbol of division and dissent. When patriotic sentiments are aroused, most voters judge specific language policies according to whether they facilitate the diffusion of English-speaking skills. Whereas political elites frequently have responded to the sensitivities of minority groups, sounding the theme of equality and characterizing support for "official English" as prejudiced and unfair, the general public has regarded English as a defining element of a vulnerable civic identity.

From Symbolism to Pragmatism

Regardless of their ethnicity, most Americans take for granted that English is the national language. Any serious challenge to this premise is bound to elicit popular resistance. But while the accusation that "official English" is tantamount to racism angers rather than converts, proclaiming a special status for English antagonizes members of linguistic minorities. In this political atmosphere, it is difficult to design language policies that enjoy widespread legitimacy.

The starting point for policymakers should be the overwhelming evidence that newcomers to America universally have striven to learn English and that within one generation most have done so. Bilingual programs that expedite this process increase economic opportunities for immigrants and speed their integration into the political community on terms that almost everyone accepts. The goals of language policy should be improving access to English, the nation's *public* language, and ensuring tolerance for the use of other languages in the *private* realm. Once bilingualism becomes a practical complement rather than a principled challenge to the dominant image of American identity, the salience of the impulses underlying the "official English" movement will diminish.

The following principles provide the framework for a language policy designed to achieve social comity rather than to win a war of symbols:

1. *Efforts to pass "official English" measures should be abandoned.* The instrumental consequences of state and local "official English" legislation are virtually nil, and in the absence of a genuine threat to the status of English, the formal subordination of other languages is mainly divisive.

2. Still, *the existence of a common language helps strengthen national identity.* The purpose of bilingual-education programs in the public schools should be to teach English as rapidly and effectively as possible. Given that the common language of international science and economics is English, improving the linguistic skills of all Americans is a vital national interest. For any particular student, bilingual education should be a transitional stage. The maintenance of one's ethnic identity, however desirable this might be, is a matter for the home and communal institutions.

3. *Current English instruction for adults is inadequate.* The expansion of adult-education programs is imperative for the social and economic integration of linguistic minorities into the American mainstream. Only if these programs are effective and readily available is it reasonable to insist on English proficiency as a condition of naturalization.

4. *The federal government should help pay for these programs.* The influx of linguistic minorities into America is largely the result of federal actions—immigration reform, refugee policy, the inability to seal the border with Mexico, and foreign-policy misadventures. But the impact of immigration falls mainly on local institutions and officials who must cope with the demands for housing,

schooling, jobs, and public assistance, and must mediate the tensions generated by the clash of unfamiliar cultural strains. Money is one solvent for these conflicts. Having called the tune, the federal government should recognize its responsibility and pay the piper.

5. *The concept of the melting pot should be revitalized.* In a society whose population constantly replenishes itself with immigrants from diverse cultures, the inculcation of a unifying civic identity is a permanent problem. The melting pot—the process of cultural assimilation that yields a people to whom America has a common meaning—remains an attractive solution. The ethos of the melting pot is universalistic and inclusive; it produces individuals who are Americans by virtue of their commitment to a democratic national creed.

The resurgence of ethnicity in the late 1960s gave rise to attacks on the melting pot and appeals for a "multicultural" version of American nationality. If multiculturalism means no more than the voluntary maintenance of a proud sense of an ethnic group's contribution to the nation's history, it fits easily into the American tradition. But if it means that there should be no single American identity, only several culturally distinct identities whose preservation requires governmental intervention, then multiculturalism implies an alien conception of the nation as a confederation of ethnic communities rather than a community of equal individuals. There will be strong public support for policies that benefit minorities only when these policies are framed in ways that affirm rather than attack the dominant conception of American identity.

If current trends in the ethnic composition of American society continue, language issues will remain on the political agenda. Harmony in diversity requires some consensus on customs and values. The United States cannot be Switzerland, the Austro-Hungarian empire, or even Canada. Our destiny is a revitalized melting pot in which all elements—indigenous and immigrant, majority and minority—intermingle to produce a new identity for all. In this process, something is given up; experience suggests that language is one aspect of the old culture that must be set aside.

OFFICIAL ENGLISH OR ENGLISH ONLY[2]

Whether English should be the official language of the United States is a debater's dream—there are no absolutely right or wrong answers. We can prove pretty conclusively that a nuclear bomb will kill people; it is somewhat harder to prove that making English our legally official language will harm anyone or to prove the opposite, that pursuing a policy of multilingualism will aid anyone. However, we can get a clearer view of the topic by avoiding the flaming rhetoric and the smoke generated from the flames and exploring the question to see what issues are involved.

"Official English" and "English Only" are apparently synonymous terms. However, the two phrases are not the same. To call for an "official" English is to call for a law specifying that English is the language which is to be used for official government functions, functions which would, of course, need to be specified in the law. Presumably, if English were declared the legally official language of the federal government, it would then be required that all federal documents would be printed in English, that federal legislative sessions would be conducted in English, perhaps even that government officials would be required to be fluent speakers and writers of English. But legislation that specifies that English be the official language of the United States need not require that English be the only language in which the government conducts its business or communicates with the public it serves. It is quite conceivable that legislation requiring that English be the official language should also require that important legislation or legislative debates be translated into the major languages in use in the United States.

Legislation requiring that English should be the *only* language used in the United States is clearly much more restrictive, and although it could have those consequences touched on in the previous paragraph, other possible consequences might arise as well, consequences not so clearly obvious. It is possible that English-only legislation could be used to prohibit children from speaking a language other than English in public places, such as

[2]Article by James C. Stalker. From *English Journal* 77:18–23 Mr '88. Copyright © 1988 by National Council of Teachers of English. Reprinted with permission.

public school playgrounds. It could mean that languages other than English could not be spoken in any public places—the street, public offices. It could mean that we must designate certain areas in which languages other than English could be used, much as we now do for cigarette smokers in some states. Such consequences may seem facetious, but they are not. Laws require or prohibit certain specified actions. A law declaring English as the only legal language must inevitably be tested in court to determine the contexts and situations in which the law operates. In California, the recently approved official-English constitutional amendment prohibits printing ballots in any language other than English; that is a specified part of the law as passed. The group that supported the amendment most vigorously, US English, has also sought the prohibition of advertisements in any language other than English, including those in the Yellow Pages, a quite legal attempt to test how far the law can be extended. In how many and what kinds of situations can the use of a language other than English be prohibited? English as an official language does not necessarily prohibit the use of any other language, although it opens the door for such a prohibition. English as the only legal language opens the prohibitive doors immediately and obviously, and in many cases the call for an official status for English is a thinly disguised call for English as the only legal language.

Clarification of the Issues

Before we consider further the practical consequences of our two possibilities—official English and English only, we need to consider the underlying concerns which have brought this question to the level of importance that it now has, and we need to separate the nonlinguistic, political issues from the linguistic ones. One of the primary expressed reasons for the call for an official English centers on bilingual programs and on Hispanic and Asian immigrants. The most common statement is that the Hispanic and Asian populations prefer not to assimilate into mainstream American culture, that they do not want to learn English or adopt traditional, mainstream cultural norms, and that bilingual programs support their desire for separateness by enabling them to maintain their native language under the guise of learning English. The emotional reactions to such a position by many people who regard themselves as "traditional, mainstream" Americans is all too predictable. Those immigrants who are different and wish to remain different should go back where they came from, go back to the culture which they hold as more valuable and dear to them than "our" culture. They should go back where they are comfortable and everyone speaks their language.

There are really three issues here: (1) the legitimacy of cultural maintenance, (2) the intention and effectiveness of bilingual programs, and (3) simple communication. For the first of these issues, we can say the obvious: that we are all culturally different in some way or another; that each of us very probably values and wishes to maintain or obtain some part of our native heritage, whatever it is; that we are all immigrants, except for Amerindians; and that we expect others to be tolerant and accepting of our Scots, Polish, Russian, or African heritage. (During periods of high immigration, claims that assimilation is not happening seem to be more prevalent. We must also remember that as a nation, we at least give lip service to the notion that our cultural diversity is one of the factors which separates the United States from many other countries in the world, one of the factors that has enabled the US to maintain an open society in the face of political, economic, and social strains which prevent other countries from realizing their full potential. We have been coping with political and cultural diversity since before the Revolution and engaging in cultural maintenance for at least that long.

The second issue, that of the intention and effectiveness of bilingual programs, should be handled as a separate problem. If bilingual programs are ineffective in teaching children English, then something should be done about the programs themselves. Passing a law directed at the official status of English is relatively unlikely to make the bilingual programs better. Outlawing the programs through an English-only law is even less likely to improve the English of the children and adults now in those programs.

The focus on bilingual programs is in part prompted by an often unarticulated fear that we will become a nation which will need interpreters in the legislature. It is a concern over communication, a concern that we might be able to deal with somewhat more objectively than the problem of cultural and political difference.

Historical Background

Language diversity was already an issue before the Revolution. As early as 1753, in a letter to a friend, Benjamin Franklin expressed the fear that German would be so prevalent in Pennsylvania that the legislature would need interpreters. . . . There were German bilingual schools in Pennsylvania during the latter half of the nineteenth century; German newspapers were common in New York and Pennsylvania, down the Ohio River valley, into Missouri and Texas.

We can get some retrospective idea of how substantial the influence of the German immigrants would have been throughout nineteenth- and early twentieth-century America, linguistically and culturally, by consulting the 1980 census, in which the number of people who reported themselves as being of German heritage was only slightly less than the number reporting themselves as being of English heritage—49.6 million English to 49.2 million German. Scottish and Irish heritage people add another 50.2 million, but many of those immigrants did not think of themselves as English, nor did they speak the same dialect.

Other language groups desired to maintain their native languages when they came to the United States, and a look into our history turns up some interesting results of that desire. The Louisiana constitution allowed the publication of laws in French, and they were so published until about seventy years ago. California (1849) and Texas allowed the publication of laws in Spanish, and New Mexico still maintained Spanish and English as official languages of the state until 1941. In 1842 Texas required the publication of its laws in German as well as Spanish and English and added Norwegian in 1858. After the Civil War, several states required the use of English as the language of instruction in the public schools, but several allowed the use of other languages in one way or another. In Louisiana, French could be used in those parishes where the French language was spoken. Hawaii allowed the use of other languages by petition. Minnesota required books in English, but explanations could be in other languages. What all of this tells us is that we have never been absolutely certain that we need to or should require that everyone speak and read and write English. On the other hand, there has been a rather constant pressure to maintain a common language, and that language has been English. German had the strongest chance to displace English; in fact, it had nearly two hundred years to do so, but it did not succeed. The conclusion that we can draw is that English is probably not seriously threatened. It has maintained its position as the common language and likely will continue to do so.

The Status of Spanish: Present and Future

The assumption that Spanish will succeed in displacing English where German did not is probably unfounded, but we must recognize that the possibility exists. However, certain conditions must prevail for that eventuality to take place. The Spanish speakers must not only want to maintain Spanish, but they must also refuse to learn any English at all. Even in those sections of the country in which there are large Spanish-speaking populations, it does not seem to be economically possible for all Spanish immigrants to remain monolingual. In fact, the evidence points to the opposite conclusion. Results from a 1976 study indicate that of 2.5 million people who spoke Spanish as their native language, 1.6 million adopted English as their principal language. Fifty per cent of the population switched from Spanish to English as their principal language. In order to offset this large loss of native speakers, Veltman calculates that Spanish-speaking women would need to produce 4.5 children each, but the average Chicano woman has only 2.9 children. A 1985 Rand Corporation study found that "more than 95 per cent of first-generation Mexican-Americans born in the United States are proficient in English and that more than half the second generation speaks no Spanish at all." Another study found that 98 per cent of Hispanic parents in Miami felt it essential that their children read and write English perfectly. In other words, Spanish speakers in the United States show a strong tendency to become English speakers, and as a result we are unlikely to become a Spanish-speaking country.

The loss of native speakers might be offset by the immigration of new Spanish speakers, but the evidence is that 50 per cent of Spanish speakers who immigrate to the US already speak some English. They obviously are not Spanish-only speakers and can be reasonably expected to learn more English. It is simply maladaptive and dysfunctional not to do so. If the only way to prevent the maintenance of Spanish among a particular part of the population is to control immigration, then we must take the bull by his horns rather than his tail. We must control immigration through restrictive immigration laws rather than by trying to control immigration through a constitutional amendment mandating English as the official language. Would such an amendment then enable us to control immigration by preventing anyone who does not speak English from migrating to the US? That would be a very interesting law indeed.

To be complete, we need to consider the possibility that the statistics I have given are inaccurate—that Spanish speakers are not learning English at any great rate, that Spanish speakers will pour into the country in such large numbers that their number will equal or exceed the number of speakers of English, and that as a consequence, we will become a country with two major languages. If that should happen, the US could also become a country socially, politically, and linguistically divided, like Canada or Sri Lanka or any of several African countries. Countries which are composed of two largely monolingual groups do seem to have more tensions that tend to pull the nation apart rather than aid it in retaining unity. It is not generally politically wise for a nation to possess two major, equally important languages, especially when each group attaches great emotional value to its own language and culture and becomes xenophobic about the other language and culture. Will passing a law declaring English as the official language prevent the rise of a second major language? Only if we also pass a set of restrictive laws, among them a law which limits immigration to those people who already speak English, and a law which prohibits the use of any language other than English.

Legislation: Effects and Alternatives

We have to question the effectiveness of these two additional laws. Limiting immigration might indeed work. . . . We have not been very effective in enforcing the immigration restrictions that we already have, and a new, more restrictive law is unlikely to accomplish any more than the current laws do.

The money for massive enforcement of current or new immigration restrictions is unlikely to materialize, so let's consider the ramifications of the other major possibility, prohibition of the use of any language other than English. If any language group, Spanish or other, chooses to maintain its language, there is precious little that we can do about it, legally or otherwise, and still maintain that we are a free country. We cannot legislate the language of the home, the street, the bar, the club, unless we are willing to violate the privacy of our people, unless we are willing to set up a cadre of language police who will ticket and arrest us if we speak something other than English. What we can do is disenfranchise all of those who have not yet learned or cannot learn English. We can exclude them from the possibility of taking part in our political system and from our schools, and because they will be uneducated, we can prevent them from benefiting from the economic system. We can insure a new oppressed minority. If that minority becomes a majority, through immigration (legal or illegal) and through birth, we will live with the consequences of our actions.

I dwelt on the German immigration into our country in the eighteenth and nineteenth centuries because that group very deliberately maintained its language and culture. Thus, those parts of the Spanish and Asian populations which are reluctant to abandon their culture and language because they had to abandon their countries for political and economic reasons are not unique to the United States. This is not a new problem. The Germans, for the most part, have eventually become users of English, not because of repressive linguistic policies or legislation, but for that most effective reason of all—utility. People learn a new language or dialect if they see that that language or dialect has high potential value for them, not because they are legally required to. The very fact that our current evidence says that more Spanish speakers are learning English than are retaining their own language is a pretty good indication that a good many of them believe English to be more useful and therefore more valuable than Spanish. English enables them to gain more than they have, to partake in the political and economic life of the United States more fully than Spanish (or Vietnamese or Chinese) does.

Our need is not to insure that everyone in the United States be a monolingual speaker of English but rather to insure that our country continues to hold its own politically and economically in the world at large. To accomplish this task, all Americans must be less provincial and less linguistically ethnocentric. English is now the predominant world language, especially in business, technology, and education, the mainstays of traditional, mainstream American culture. Because of the world-wide importance of English as an international language, it is unlikely that the United States will lose English as its common language at a time when other countries are seeking more speakers of English and teaching their own populations English. However, we will need people who can speak the languages of other countries. For the United States to continue to be an important economic and political power in the world, Americans of whatever variety will need two languages—their first language and English, or English and a second language. English is indeed a world language, but as every international tourist or business traveler learns, not everyone in the world speaks English. Rather than eliminate the second language of our immigrants, we need to help them learn English and maintain that valuable resource they already have, the use of a second language, and we need to teach our native English speakers a second language.

The United States has always been a polyglot country. It is part of our strength. It is unlikely that nonnative speakers of English, be they immigrants or born here, will remain monolingual, because they need English to talk with other Americans whose native language is not English and with other people in the world who do not speak Vietnamese or Spanish or French or Arabic or whatever. Multilingualism in a country is potentially dangerous only if it becomes the rallying point for cultural divisiveness. Otherwise, it is a benefit of great economic and political value.

Aside from the purely utilitarian economic value of knowing more than one language, there is evidence that knowing a second language increases our abilities to use our first language. People who know two languages generally perform better on tests of verbal ability administered in their native language than do monolingual speakers. That is to say, if your native language is English, and you learn Japanese, you will perform better on tests which measure your knowledge of and abilities in English. Parents who know and accept the research that shows that "bilingual youngsters are more imaginative, better with abstract notions and more flexible in their thinking" are enrolling their children in private language programs to give them the advantage that bilingual programs give other groups of children.

Conclusion

Neither our Congress nor any other national legislature has ever had much success in legislating morals or beliefs. . . . Rather than taking the path of linguistic legislation, we are much more likely to be successful in maintaining a common language in the United States by pursuing the American tradition of persuasion and demonstration. The very fact that English speakers (whether English is their first or second language) are economically and politically more powerful than non-English speakers is a better argument for learning English than an argument based on the fact that English is the official or only language of the United States. . . .

I have tried to point out some distinctions here, perhaps the most important of which is that *official, only,* and *common* are not synonymous when coupled with *English.* A great many of us wish to maintain English as the *common* language of the United States, but that goal need not, and probably should not, entail legislating English as the *only* language or the official language. The problems that we have as a multilingual society have been with us since at least 1753 when Benjamin Franklin noted them, and we have managed to overcome them or turn them to our advantage without depriving anyone of the freedom of speech that we value so highly. There are distinct advantages for our culture, for our children, and for each of us individually to be multilingual, especially if we all share a language in common. If we are concerned about the quality and intent of bilingual programs or about the effects of our immigration policies, let's be direct and honest and focus on those and not pretend that legislating language choice will improve or change bilingual programs or slow immigration.

OFFICIAL ENGLISH ISN'T AS GOOD AS IT SOUNDS[3]

We take the English language for granted, and have for the better part of 200 years. Seldom has it been a symbol of national pride, a stake in ethnic strife, or an issue for legislative debate. Unlike many countries, the U.S. has avoided debilitating conflicts over languages. Government has traditionally left the choice of language to the people, rather than mandating it by law.

Paradoxically, this laissez-faire attitude has fostered the most massive language shift in recorded history—"Babel in reverse," in the words of linguist Einar Haugen—as millions of immigrants embraced English. "The United States has probably been the home of more bilingual speakers than any other country in the world," Haugen says. And yet, it remains among the most monolingual.

Today, growing numbers of Americans seem determined to keep it that way. This decade has witnessed the birth of a new

[3]Article by James Crawford. From *The American School Board Journal* 176:41–44 Mr '89. Copyright © 1989 by The American School Board Journal. Reprinted with permission.

political phenomenon: a movement for the so-called "legal protection of English" and against what one advocate has termed "the mindless drift toward a bilingual society."

It is a movement few school boards—given the increasing linguistic diversity of the students they serve—can afford to ignore. The "official English" movement threatens to undermine guarantees of bilingual services to students with limited proficiency in English. And it has the potential to spark the kind of language strife the U.S. has so far avoided.

Make It Official?

In 1981, for the first time, Congress entertained a proposal to declare English the official language of the U.S. Since then, more than 40 states have considered the idea; by the end of 1988, 16 had adopted official-English measures—most recently, Arizona, Colorado, and Florida through ballot initiatives last fall.

Since 1983, a Washington, D.C., lobbying group known as U.S. English has spent nearly $20 million on behalf of this campaign. Its stated goal: an amendment to the U.S. Constitution making English the country's official language.

So far, most federal legislators have been wary of the official-English idea. As Representative Albert Bustamante (D-Tex.) observed in a hearing last May: "Given the fact that English is our national language, we question the need to recognize the obvious. After all, amending our Constitution is a serious matter. Since the ratification of the Bill of Rights in 1791, the nation has made only 16 changes in the Constitution. . . . If [official English] is a symbolic measure with no impact whatsoever on our rights, then it is a frivolous exercise. If it restricts civil rights on the basis of one's proficiency in English, then it is a divisive and dangerous amendment."

Indeed, considering that we have gotten by without an official tongue since 1787, do we really need one now? It's not as though an official language has been sorely missed: In a recent survey conducted by Hearst Newspapers, 64 percent of respondents assumed that English already enjoyed constitutional status.

What would an English-language amendment accomplish? Is the intent to celebrate English—or to restrict the use of other languages? Would it bring newcomers into the mainstream—or erect discriminatory barriers? Will the "English-only" campaign help or hurt relations among ethnic groups?

U.S. English, in published materials, reasons as follows: "Historically, our shared language has been our common meeting ground and our strongest bond," providing a means for Americans of diverse backgrounds to settle their differences. "But now English is under attack. . . . Record immigration, concentrated in fewer language groups, is reinforcing language segregation." Government has erected "barriers to assimilation" with misguided programs like bilingual education, which discourages children from learning English. Ethnic leaders, notably Hispanics, are espousing "language separatism." Unless we act now to legislate "the primacy of English," we risk "the agonies of language polarization" experienced by such countries as Canada.

Myths and Misconceptions

Many voters, on hearing these arguments for the first time, have found them persuasive. And yet, U.S. English has mustered little evidence to support them. Because an explicit politics of language has been rare here, few Americans are well informed about official English and its implications. It has been a campaign fueled by symbolism—a combination of patriotic myths, ethnic stereotypes, and misconceptions about language:

Myth 1: English is the tie that binds. Supporters of an English-language amendment argue that English is the "social glue" that holds the U.S. together—a claim that would have seemed strange to our country's founders. As Harvard sociologist Nathan Glazer explains, early Americans envisioned a new type of nationhood "defined by commitment to ideals . . . rather than by ethnicity." Until 1906 there was no English-speaking requirement for naturalization; to become a U.S. citizen, it was sufficient to be of good character and to swear allegiance to the Constitution.

The framers of that document took no action to protect or promote English, although our common language was, if anything, more threatened then than now. German Americans—whose preference for their native tongue drew criticism from Benjamin Franklin—made up 8.7 percent of the U.S. population in the 1790 census. (By comparison, Hispanics represented 8.1 percent in 1988.)

Evidence strongly suggests that our lack of an official tongue was no oversight. The hope and expectation was that non-English-speakers would assimilate—but without coercion. Benjamin Rush proposed to encourage the process with a bilingual college, which, he argued, would "open the eyes of the Germans to a sense of the importance and utility of the English language and become perhaps the only possible means, consistent with their liberty, of spreading a knowledge of the English language among them."

Myth 2: Earlier immigrants learned English without special programs. Rush's German College never received federal funding. But during the 19th century, at least a dozen states and territories passed laws authorizing bilingual public schooling. In other areas where ethnic minorities had political clout, dual-language instruction was common without legal sanction.

By the beginning of this century, 600,000 children—or approximately 4 percent of the U.S. elementary school population, public and parochial—were receiving part or all of their instruction in the German language, according to historian Heinz Kloss. For substantial numbers of other students, French, Spanish, or Norwegian was the medium of instruction. And thanks to pressure from immigrant communities, Polish, Czech, Italian, and Dutch were frequently offered as school subjects.

Bilingual programs were largely dismantled during the World War I era, when fears about "hyphenated Americans" (that is, citizens of German ancestry) made speaking English an emblem of political loyalty. Coercive language laws were enacted on a large scale for the first time, and by 1919, a majority of states had adopted English as the sole language of instruction. Several banned the teaching of foreign languages in the elementary grades; such statutes were later ruled unconstitutional by the U.S. Supreme Court in *Meyer v. Nebraska*.

Myth 3: Today's language minorities are failing to assimilate. This charge is nothing new: In 1911, the federal Dillingham Commission accused the "new immigrants" of that time—the Italians, Jews, and Slavs—of failing to learn English as quickly as the German and Scandinavian immigrants who arrived before them. In the 1980s, similar complaints are being lodged against Hispanics and Asians.

Immigration by non-English-speakers has increased noticeably in the past two decades. Language minorities are more visible—many are racial minorities as well—and more audible than before. Showing little reverence for the Melting Pot tradition, newcomers like the Cubans in Miami and the Taiwanese in southern California seem to be "making it" without giving up their own languages and cultures.

There is no indication, however, that today's immigrants are indifferent to English. Los Angeles has had up to 40,000 adults on waiting lists for instruction in English as a second language. Demand is so great that these classes now operate 24 hours a day.

Far from slowing down, in fact, linguistic assimilation appears to be accelerating. Demographer Calvin Veltman reported in 1988 that Hispanic newcomers are approaching a two-generation model of "anglicization," or shift to English dominance, as compared with the three-generation pattern of previous immigrants. After 15 years in this country, 75 percent of Spanish-speaking immigrants use English on a daily basis, Veltman found, and 70 percent of their children become English speakers for all practical purposes.

In a 1983 study analyzing the U.S. Department of Education's High School and Beyond data base, Veltman concluded that bilingual education has virtually no effect in slowing down the anglicization process. Spanish speakers are somewhat more likely to retain their native tongue than other groups, according to Veltman's research. But bilingualism is not the same as resistance to English. Polled in 1985, 98 percent of Hispanic parents in Miami said it was essential for their children to read and write English perfectly (only 94 percent of Anglo parents said the same).

Myth 4: Many nations recognize an official language because bilingual societies are divided societies. In arguing that an official-English amendment is hardly a radical idea, U.S. English often points to its own 1986 survey of world constitutions. Conducted by Rutgers University law professor Albert Blaustein, the study reported that 64 of 161 countries had official language provisions. But the group neglects to mention another significant finding: Forty-five of those constitutions recognize the rights of more than one language group, either through official status or guarantees against discrimination.

In themselves, differences of language no more "cause" social divisions than do other salient features of human diversity, such as race, religion, or cultural heritage. For example, Switzerland's German, French, Italian, and Romansh-speaking communities have long coexisted peacefully on the basis of equality. By contrast, Canada's oft-cited conflicts reflect a history of second-class citizenship for French speakers. Before the 1960s, language served as a pervasive tool of economic and political discrimination against one-quarter of Canada's population. Official bilingualism has been an attempt to restore equal access to government services.

Although such provisions are not always sufficient to defuse
tensions over language, restrictive legislation is likely to exacer-
bate the tensions. Quebec's French-only laws of the 1970s—a clas-
sic overreaction to cultural repression—trampled the civil liberties of English speakers and left a strong impression on many
people in the U.S. Some here ask whether granting demands for
bilingual services might encourage Hispanic separatism in the
U.S.

Consider Dade County, Florida, where a Hispanic takeover
often is forecast. In 1973, Dade County passed a ceremonial resolution declaring itself bilingual and bicultural. The little-noticed
measure was used primarily to attract Latin American investors to
South Florida. But in 1980, shortly after the Mariel boatlift
brought a new wave of Cuban refugees, voters enacted a blanket
anti-bilingual ordinance that prohibited any public use of languages other than English. Health and emergency services were
later exempted, but the ban remains largely in place—extending
even to Spanish-language signs at bus stops in Cuban neighborhoods.

Such a repressive response to diversity, as Canada's experience demonstrates, is an efficient way to encourage language
strife. Contrary to its stated goals, that is what today's English-
only movement is beginning to deliver.

What It Would Mean

The practical impact of an official English amendment has
been the subject of intense speculation and debate, complicated
by the variety of proposals now pending. Some versions of official
English would forbid all levels of government—federal, state, and
local—from providing services or conducting business in other
languages, with a few exceptions for public safety and education.

Other proposals are one-liners, simply declaring English to be
the official language and leaving the interpretation to judges and
legislators. In states where such laws or amendments have passed,
courts have tended to regard them as purely symbolic.

California's Proposition 63, approved by the voters in 1986,
instructed the state legislature to "make no law which diminishes
or ignores the role of English." It also invited lawsuits by any
taxpayer to enforce this provision. . . .

So far, the most significant effects of Proposition 63 have
been indirect. It created a political climate in which Governor

George Deukmejian, a Republican, twice vetoed legislation to extend the state's bilingual education law. Previously, California had the most extensive guarantees in the U.S. for students of limited English proficiency. Now it has none, although most school systems maintain the same bilingual programs as before.

Edward Chen, an attorney who has monitored Proposition 63 for the American Civil Liberties Union, says that "overall, we've seen a rising intolerance." He reports an increase in arbitrary English-only rules in the workplace—unrelated to business necessity—which violate guidelines of the U.S. Equal Employment Opportunity Commission. Chen also reports moves to restrict business signs in languages other than English.

In Arizona . . . voters adopted the most restrictive official-English measure to date. Approved by less than 1 percent of the vote, Proposition 106 is a constitutional amendment that leaves few loopholes:

"This State and all political subdivisions of this State shall act in English and no other language. . . . This Article applies to: (i) the legislative, executive, and judicial branches of government; (ii) all political subdivisions, departments, agencies, organizations, and instrumentalities of this State, including local governments and municipalities; (iii) all statutes, ordinances, rules, orders, programs, and policies; (iv) all government officials and employees during the performance of government business."

The measure allows exceptions "to teach a student a foreign language" and for bilingual education "to provide as rapid as possible a transition to English." But Arizona educators fear the amendment will be disastrous for children whose English proficiency is limited. One Tucson teacher predicts that Proposition 106 will outlaw her school's bilingual program—which develops students' native-language skills beyond the point at which they become proficient in English—and that it will prohibit her, as a public employee, from communicating with the majority of parents, who speak only Spanish.

When or if such effects will be felt remains unclear. Shortly after Proposition 106 passed, Governor Rose Mofford, a Democrat, announced she would refuse to enforce it. Confusion reigned about how to interpret the provision. The only certainty was litigation over its constitutionality. . . .

ENGLISH VS. SPANISH IN SOUTH
FLORIDA[4]

With its large Spanish-speaking population, Florida's Dade
County (Miami) has long been a barometer of popular opinion
about bilingualism. Over the years, local sentiment on the subject
has gone from one extreme to the other and then back again.

In 1973, the County Commission unanimously adopted a resolution formally declaring the county to be bilingual, with Spanish joining English as a second official language. The commission
also created a department of bilingual and bicultural affairs to
implement the resolution. At that time, the county's population
was about 1.3 million, including 450,000 Hispanics.

Seven years later, Dade County was jolted by the sudden influx of 125,000 mostly poor Cuban refugees during the Mariel
boatlift. By then, the county's Hispanic population had grown to
650,000, or 41 percent of the total, alarming many longtime,
English-speaking residents who feared loss of their accustomed
majority status. Capitalizing on that feeling, a group called Citizens of Dade United pressed for a referendum reversing the
1973 resolution. Voters approved the proposal by a 3-2 margin in
November 1980.

The ballot measure did more than just overturn the earlier
vote by the County Commission. It also declared that, "The expenditure of county funds for the purpose of utilizing any language other than English, or promoting any culture than that of
the United States, is prohibited."

Critics complained the wording was vague and legally confus-
ing. "What is United States culture?" asked Dade County Attorney Robert A. Ginsburg. "After all, Florida was discovered by
Ponce de Leon, and certainly Spanish was spoken here long before English."

Though the 1980 law designated English as Dade County's
language, it permitted Spanish for such government services as
911 emergency calls, voter-education programs and aid to the
elderly. And it imposed no restrictions on the use of languages

[4]Article from *CQ Researcher* 3:708 Ag 13 '93. Copyright © 1993 by CQ Researcher. Reprinted with permission.

other than English at work, home or in public places. But the very existence of the law rankled Miami-area Hispanics, who regarded it as a calculated affront to their culture.

In another turnabout, county commissioners unanimously voted this May [1993] to strike down the 1980 language ordinance. Citizens of Dade United immediately served notice that it planned to challenge the action in court. "There are 150 [ethnic] groups out there," said Enos Schera, the group's vice president, "and I'll be damned if we are going to spend money just for Spanish-speakers." On Aug. 5 [1993], however, a Florida judge upheld the commission's repeal of the ordinance.

The language issue has surfaced in many other areas besides Dade County. According to the anti-bilingualism group U.S. English, 19 states now recognize English as their official language, and several others are considering similar action.

For the most part, these laws, resolutions and constitutional amendments amount only to symbolic statements. Susannah D. A. MacKaye, a California teacher of English as a second language, says they spring from two common assumptions—"that bilingualism or biculturalism is inherently divisive and the assumption that the essential common thread of the multiethnic American society is the English language." She notes, "Many editorials point to language as the only thread in the social fabric, and other shared values, such as democracy, fall away or go unnoted."

Groups that favor making English the official U.S. language accuse supporters of bilingual education of trying to have it both ways. In a July 1986 op-ed page column in *USA Today,* then-U.S. English Executive Director Gerda Bikales wrote: "Those who tell us the palpable erosion of English is a matter of little concern don't convince anyone when they . . . [i]nsist that a common language is *not* at the foundation of U.S. unity and social cohesion, while blatantly using the Spanish language to unify the very diverse Spanish-speaking populations in the USA."

In MacKaye's opinion, Bikales' comments "exemplify how, paradoxically, language as common bond can simultaneously unify and divide. By linguistically unifying one group in opposition to another, the common bond of language can function as a dividing force."

WHITE SUPREMACY OR APPLE PIE?: THE POLITICS OF MAKING ENGLISH THE OFFICIAL LANGUAGE OF ARIZONA[5]

Nazis goosestop across your TV screen. American flags on bumperstickers appear in front of you in traffic jams. A picture-perfect older white male looks out at you from your TV screen and proudly explains how he learned English when he first came to this country.

Do you remember?

These images appeared frequently the few days before the vote on Proposition 106, the amendment to make English the official language of Arizona. Some images were arresting and some unexpected. For example, were the flag images only on bumperstickers of those who opposed 106? No. They were on those of the proponents also.

The Arizona campaign for Proposition 106 made clear to those looking and listening that language choice is a "political issue," not because people were asked to cast a vote but because when people anywhere elect one language to a status different from another language they also elect the speakers of that language to a different status.

How can that be? Proponents of 106 told us that making English the official language was really no different from choosing a state bird or flower, so why should opponents associate images of Nazis with the legislation? Proponents argued that since English is the common language of the nation, why not recognize that fact legally? The law would only be a recognition of existing conditions. They claimed also that language is a neutral code for communication like Morse code, and the selection of English merely expedient. For example, during a roundtable discussion at Arizona State University in March, 1987, Stanley Diamond, Chairman of U.S. English (a national organization advocating official English) said that if more people in the United States spoke Spanish than English, then Spanish should be declared the official language.

[5]Article by Karen L. Adams, Professor of English at Arizona State University, Tempe. From *Arizona English Bulletin* 33:23–29 Wtr '92. Copyright © 1992 by the Arizona English Teachers Association. Reprinted with permission.

But a "symbolic" law is not a neutral one especially when the symbol is language. Language itself is a symbol, not the neutral code that people claim. Language is a symbol of one's social identity, including one's friends, one's family, one's ethnicity, one's race, one's class, one's gender role identification, one's religion, and one's occupation. It is a symbol of all social identities and relationships mediated by language. By making English the official language of Arizona or the United States, one gives it privileges as a symbol of social identity above all others.

The images we saw before the election in 1988 exemplify the kinds of symbols proponents and opponents attributed to the amendment to make English the official language of Arizona. The strength of those images relates directly to the intensity of feelings proponents and opponents had and still have about the amendment.

The Nazi image found in the advertisements against Proposition 106 came from a newspaper article by James Crawford which appeared in various valley newspapers on October 30, 1988. Crawford's article detailed the links of some leaders and financial backers of national organizations advocating officialization to organizations advocating immigration restrictions and population control. One group provided financial backing to an immigration reform group headed from 1981–86 by John Tanton who in 1988 was the chair of U.S. English. This group, the Pioneer Fund, had included eugenics—control of human gene pools—among their strategies for population control. In the late 1930's they supported Hitler's strategy of forced sterilization for populations considered inferior by Nazis. In the 1970's, this group also supported research by William Shockley and Arthur Jensen to prove the intellectual inferiority of African-Americans. This information was relevant for the Arizona campaign because Arizonans for Official English, the group supporting Proposition 106, is the Arizona affiliate of U.S. English, and Arizonans for Official English were receiving financial help from the parent organization during the campaign.

Crawford's article also quoted from a memo written by John Tanton, then chair of U.S. English, which asked questions such as "will the present majority peaceably hand over its political power to a group that is simply more fertile?" The clear anti-Hispanic tone of the memo caused Linda Chavez, a conservative Republican Hispanic and the president of U.S. English, to resign from the group after its release in October 1988. Other anti-Hispanic

indexes could be found in U.S. English's newsletters and statements by supporters. For example, there was a preponderance of
articles in U.S. English's newsletters attacking Hispanics as the
source of language difficulties in the U.S. And a proponent of
official English and an appointee to the U.S. Department of Education, R. E. Butler, wrote a research paper stating that bilingual
education fed the Hispanic ideal of a homeland (Aztlan) which
would include parts of the Southwest and, therefore, had national
security implications.

Given these revelations one can understand why many non-
white ethic groups, and white ones too, had reason to view an
official English amendment as a symbol of more sinister feelings
among some of the supporters. These concerns found further
justification in the knowledge that earlier legislative attempts to
give English official status also involved outlawing the use of other languages and were open about their ethnic and racial bias. See
for example the 1920's *Meyer v. Nebraska* case. The assumption
was that similar motives were at work in 1988, but more cleverly
concealed.

For the proponents of official English, not recognizing the
special status of English, or not learning to speak it and maintaining non-English languages, meant the rejection of "American"
values and their possible loss. Opponents saw the imposition of
official English as the potential destruction of their race and culture. On either side, the law was not seen as merely the equivalent
of naming a state bird.

Other objections to Proposition 106 focused on the rights and
status of non-native English speakers. For many Arizona communities, the claim for special status for English was insulting since
their non-English speaking communities have been here long before the English speaking ones. These communities include not
only Native American ones but also certain Hispanic communities. Even the U.S. Congress has recognized the irony of placing
English above indigenous languages. Since the increase in official
English language laws at the state level and the continued lobbying for a federal English Language Amendment, Congress has
passed legislation protecting indigenous language in the form of
the Native American Language Rights Act passed as part of the
Tribally Controlled Community College Act of October 12, 1990.
Many Native American communities have also developed their
own language policies to counter pressure from omnipresent English use and the official English movement.

Among the opponents of official English in Arizona there was also true concern for the kinds of bilingual services that would be eliminated with the passage of an official English amendment. Many vital services—hospital, police and fire emergency numbers, driver's license tests, employment and unemployment applications—are available in bilingual or trilingual format. To lose these services would be devastating for those who rely on them, and . . . loss of these services is not only anti-Hispanic and anti-ethnic minorities but also anti-elderly and anti-female. The elderly and women are more likely to maintain their native language since their contacts in the wider English speaking community are often more restricted. To allay opponents' fears on this issue, the Arizona amendment was hedged with safeguards for several types of services although not all. The amendment still meant it would be difficult for citizens to communicate with their government.

Even the protection of some bilingual rights at the state level in Arizona is not what it appears. State Constitution amendments only affect state issues, (much to the disappointment expressed by some supporters on post-election editorial pages), but the national strategy of proponents is to pass enough state legislation so that a national amendment (the ELA—English Language Amendment) can be passed. Bilingual rights might not fare as well nationally since the U.S. English's newsletter makes it clear that they perceive bilingual education, bilingual ballots, and other policies as retarding language shift to English and encouraging the maintenance of non-English languages.

The American flags on opponents' bumper stickers must have seemed inappropriate to supporters of the proposition who view those opposing official English as people who steadfastly refuse to learn English and to assimilate into the American way of life. So why do opponents to official English use the flag as a symbol? Is a lack of an official English policy as American as apple pie?

That appears to be the case. The founders of the U.S. government had long debates about the issue of an official language and the creation of a language academy like those in France and Spain. The new nation was linguistically diverse with German speakers being at least 6% of the population, but

. . . the founding fathers made clear their choice not to designate a national tongue . . . (they) promoted respect for diversity of languages . . . (and they) had an almost unfailing conviction that the pragmatic and universal appeals and functions of the English language would establish it as the national tongue in practice . . . Furthermore, (they) believed the individual's freedoms to make language choices and changes represented a far more valuable political asset to the new nation than did a state decision to remove these freedoms from the individual.

At a more personal level, opponents to the amendment associate the U.S. flag with their viewpoint because of their own patriotism. Hispanic organizations such as LULAC and MALDEF and some Asian American organizations see no conflict in a desire to value their culture and its language while at the same time being devoted American citizens who serve their country well in the government and armed services. This also applies to the American Indian Nations whose people have proud records of service and include the Navajo code talkers who helped win WWII.

Not surprisingly, the proponents of official English consider their position equally "apple pie" and American flag. They perceive among the growing non-white population a large number who are not English speaking and worse yet who appear not to want to become English speaking. They see them demanding and receiving special language treatment not given to earlier immigrants. Of particular concern to proponents are bilingual policies especially in education and in voting rights legislation which they think encourage non-English language maintenance and discourage the acquisition of English.

These concerns, deserve serious consideration. Let's turn first to the perception that recent immigrants are not learning English. A steady influx of immigrants from non-English speaking countries regularly introduces non-English speaking populations. However, the consensus of studies done on these populations as they continue to live in the United States is that they become fluent in English and lose their skill in their native languages at approximately the same rate as earlier immigrant groups.

The lure of English is great even if its acquisition does not entail all that proponents say it will such as better occupational opportunities. English on both a national and international level is a highly useful language. Rather than refusing to learn English, many non-English speakers find themselves on long waiting lists for English language courses because there are not enough classes and teachers. Contrary to the perceptions of proponents of official English, special efforts are needed to help people maintain their Navajo, Hopi and Zuni. This is also true for other languages such as Tagalog, Thai, and even Spanish. Since skill in another language is an economic resource as well as an intellectual one, maintenance is important.

Let's consider another perception of proponents of official English, i.e., that bilingual education programs fail because they discourage students from learning English and are expensive. Proponents argue that immersion style programs worked for earlier immigrants and will now. Hence the TV advertisements of older immigrants describing their language learning experiences. Both proponents and opponents point to research on bilingual education programs to prove their points because the evaluation of such programs has not been uniform. However, one of the most comprehensive studies of immersion, early-exit and late-exit transitional bilingual programs has recently been released.

Great care was taken to study comparable programs and all indications are that neither early-exit programs (where children enter English-only classrooms in two or three years) nor late-exit bilingual programs (where children may stay in a bilingual classroom until sixth grade) negatively effect language acquisition. Moreover, students in immersion programs (where almost all teaching is in English) and those in early-exit programs were kept in the programs for longer than required to improve their skills, suggesting that these two programs may not have been as effective as desired. On the other hand, certain positive results, for example, in math achievement, can be found in the late-exit programs but not in the other two programs. Issues of expense do not seem of great importance if late-exit bilingual programs improve students' educational achievement.

Some supporters of official English are genuinely concerned about the rights of non-English speaking populations. For example, a liberal area in California voted for an advisory policy against multilingual ballots. They were convinced by official English information that such ballots gave politicians who spoke minority languages control over information that voters received. Again while the motivation was understandable concern, the vote was based on a lack of understanding of the workings of multilingual communities where information from English speaking groups is spread by bilingual speakers.

Minority voters are concerned about issues of quality education and equal access to the American economy. And when lobbying groups convince them that official English will somehow improve their opportunities, they may vote for it, but typically not when they learn the intent to eliminate bilingual education and services. Unfortunately organizations such as U.S. English have long been neglectful of supporting education in English. Only after criticism by opponents noting that the organization was more interested in limiting other languages than in helping people learn English did the organization start supporting limited projects to teach English.

Another area of concern among proponents is the belief that the existence of many languages within one country is correlated with civil strife. Canada and other countries are used as examples. In this argument, encouraging multiple languages means weakening the U.S. . . . Certainly no one wants to encourage civil strife; enough other problems already exist. But we need to ask what is the likelihood that the present language situation will cause strife.

Surveys of the nations of the world indicate that there are few monolingual nations, and in multilingual countries there are only a few where conflicts have linguistic overtones. Another study by Fishman and Solano (1989) of 130 nations did not find language issues a factor in civil strife. The factors that contributed to civil strife were a combination of deprivation, authoritarianism, and modernization. When these factors exist, language and other cultural factors such as religion and race are often exploited to mobilize people to support one side or the other. Not all proponents of official English believe such studies, but we need to recognize that conflict can exist in countries which are monolingual, e.g., our own civil war, and multilingualism does not of necessity lead to conflict.

Proponents are also concerned about protecting the rights of English speakers. *The U.S. English Newsletter* reports cases of discrimination against English speakers in the workplace and elsewhere. Ironically, these are the same concerns that opponents of official English have. The opponents also point to what seem to be increases in discrimination since the passage of official English legislation in some states. Both proponents and opponents seek to secure language and individual rights but each group sees the exact opposite effect in official English language legislation.

The official English movement is not likely to go away. U.S. English is still actively pushing for a federal language amendment as well as for state legislation. . . .

Several states now have a policy on official English, so it is important to look seriously at these cases to see if making it official may not create as many problems as it solves and whether the problems it claims to solve are solved or exist in the first place. The founders of the U.S.A. were wise about many issues. Perhaps we should follow their lead and let English continue to win people over because of its role not only as the language of the majority but also as a language of wider communication with world-wide status. This no-policy policy worked before and still works according to recent studies.

AGAINST ENGLISH ONLY[6]

Describing the law as too broad and a violation of the First Amendment's right of free speech, U.S. District Judge Paul Rosenblatt struck down Arizona's controversial, voter-approved English Language Amendment.

"This verifies what we were telling the voters all along—that it was unconstitutional," exults Manny Mejía, a member of the Arizona steering committee that opposed the English Only law.

"It sends the message to other states that the whole notion that these measures are merely symbolic is false. They do take away the freedom of speech," adds state Rep. Armando Ruiz, a southeast Phoenix Democrat.

Gov. Rose Mofford—the object of the lawsuit—says she will not be appealing the decision, which was handed down February 6, citing that the amendment was "flawed from the beginning." The 1988 initiative, sponsored by the organization "Arizona for Official English," was narrowly approved 580,830 to 569,993. The amendment to the Arizona Constitution required state and county governments to conduct their business in English, with the exception of public health, safety, and education matters, and "to protect the rights of criminal defendants or victims of crime." It also provided enforcement powers, granting persons the right to bring suit to endorse the amendment.

The ruling came about as a result of a lawsuit filed by María Yñíguez, of Tempe, a State Department of Administration employee, two days after the passage of the initiative. Yñíguez, who evaluates and arbitrates medical malpractice claims, charged that the law inhibited her right to free speech and prevented her from carrying out her job.

[6]Article by Roberto Rodriguez, staffwriter, from *Hispanic* 18 Ap '90. Copyright © 1990 by Hispanic. Reprinted with permission.

"A state may not require that its officers and employees relinquish rights guaranteed them by the First Amendment as a condition of public employment," the judge wrote in his 21-page opinion.

Katherine Ely, communications coordinator of U.S. English, a Washington, D.C.-based umbrella group for the English Only movement, stated that the organization is considering petitioning the court for the right to intervene—so as to file an appeal.

"We disagree with the finding of the judge. He made his decision on the premise that the woman [Yñíguez] was prohibited from speaking Spanish—and that the state cannot restrict the activities of its employees. That's not the case."

Elated with the decision, Martha Jiménez, an attorney for the Mexican American Legal Defense and Educational Fund, calls it "a decision whose time has come," adding that "we [Hispanics] will no longer allow bigotry to be couched in patriotism."

ENGLISH-ONLY LABELS OK, COURT RULES[7]

In a decision with far-reaching significance for immigrants, the California Supreme Court ruled that over-the-counter drugs do not have to include warning labels in languages other than English.

The ruling is the nation's first by a state's highest court to address whether product manufacturers must include warnings in foreign languages, lawyers said.

By a unanimous vote, the court ruled Thursday against Jorge Ramirez of Modesto, now 8 years old. Lawyers for the boy said he was left blind, mentally retarded and a quadriplegic after his Spanish-speaking mother gave him aspirin when he was 4 months old. The bottle of St. Joseph Aspirin for Children included a warning that the dosage for children under 2 should be directed by a doctor.

"Although warnings in English are expressly required" for non-prescription drugs, Justice Joyce Kennard wrote, "no Cali-

[7]Article by Harriet Chiang, staffwriter, from the *San Francisco Chronicle* D 10 '93. Copyright © 1993 by San Francisco Chronicle. Reprinted with permission.

fornia statute requires label or package warnings in any other language."

The court said that any changes in the law must come from the Legislature, which has passed laws requiring information in other languages for candidates' ballot statements, food stamp applications and other documents.

After the decision, aspirin manufacturer Scheiring-Plough HealthCare of New Jersey said in a statement that the court "correctly recognized the importance of the FDA regulatory process and the state Legislature's role" in regulating labeling requirements.

Irma Rodriguez, an attorney with the Mexican American Legal Defense and Educational Fund in Los Angeles, called the decision an affront to immigrants. The decision means "that if you don't speak English, you have less protection as a consumer," she said.

"The California Supreme Court has diluted the ability of a non-English-speaking consumer to sue and be compensated for a manufacturer's wrong," Rodriguez said.

Hispanic groups had watched the case closely because Scheiring-Plough had advertised its product heavily on Spanish-speaking television and radio stations.

III. SOCIAL, CULTURAL, AND ECONOMIC IMPLICATIONS

EDITOR'S INTRODUCTION

The changing face of American society has been one of the factors in the conflict over language. Increased immigration from previously restricted regions of the world has brought not only differences in language, values, and cultural backgrounds, but also increased competition in the educational system and the marketplace. These developments have spurred the language debate to its current level.

The first article, by Gary Imhoff and Gerda Bikales from *USA Today,* explores the notion that, like religion, language is a part of culture and heritage. The responsibility of culture and heritage preservation, they write, lies not with the government but with the individual and should therefore be a matter of individual choice. A movement to declare an official language of the United States should not be viewed as racist, but rather an attempt to eliminate the "separatist" attitude which many observers feel the bilingual movement has fostered among our immigrants.

In an article titled "English in a Multicultural America," Dennis Baron questions why an official English law is necessary as long as today's immigrants appear to be following the same pattern as earlier generations in assimilating into the culture. Baron compares the history of German-speaking immigrants in the eighteenth century with that of Spanish-speaking immigrants today, pointing out that in both cases the younger people in the immigrant communities adopted English and abandoned their other language at an equal rate, obviating the need for a language amendment.

Mark Halton, writing in *The Christian Century,* suggests a gentler approach to assimilating immigrants into American society than those advocated by English-only proponents but producing the same results. The author feels that the current sensitivity toward the customs and language of different cultures is smoothing the path of acceptance. Moreover, the assimilation process is hastened by the knowledge on the part of immigrants that a command of English is necessary for success in school and career.

The last two articles focus on the issue of language in the workplace. William E. Lissy, writing in *Supervision,* describes several recent court rulings in support of Equal Opportunity Commission guidelines that make it illegal to prohibit employees from speaking a language other than English. The second article, from *CQ Researcher,* describes programs instituted by companies to help non-English speaking employees integrate into the workplace and ensure their success.

THE BATTLE OVER PRESERVING THE ENGLISH LANGUAGE[1]

The constitution of Spain has a majestic provision: "Castilian is the official Spanish language of the state. All Spaniards have the duty to know it and the right to use it." It is a provision worth examining in the light of the current debate in the U.S. over both bilingual education and the proposed English Language Amendment to the Constitution.

On first reading, "the right to use it" does not appear to grant anything very significant. After all, a language is a difficult thing to prescribe or to restrict. A language is available to anyone who expends the effort to learn it. Does this clause, then, grant anything? Is granting the right to speak a language any more significant than granting the right to breathe air? This clause recognizes something not generally acknowledged—that the language of the nation is the most valuable gift the state has to bestow on its citizens. It is the ability to communicate with one's fellows. It is the key to belonging, to becoming a full member of the polity.

However, it is the first part of the provision that would cause the most controversy in the U.S.: "the duty to know it." In past years, there would have been no doubt about this duty. It was unquestioned that both citizens of the U.S. and those who migrated to this country would learn English and use it in their public lives. Yet, in the past few years, both this duty and the

[1]Article by Gary Imhoff and Gerda Bikales. From USA Today Ja '87. Copyright © 1987 by USA Today. Reprinted by permission.

desirability of English-language unity have been sharply questioned and even denied by many ethnic spokesmen and politicians.

The American Constitution currently has no provision that gives English the status of an official language equivalent to Castilian in Spain. A constitutional English Language Amendment (ELA) to make English the official language of the U.S. was originally introduced in the Senate in April, 1981, by former Sen. S. I. Hayakawa (R.-Calif.) and is currently sponsored by Sen. Steve Symms (R.-Idaho). It is rather less sweeping than the Spanish provision, since it would impose no duty on the people to learn English and would not infringe upon anyone's right to use other languages. In one sense, therefore, it would make no practical changes. As Sen. Quentin Burdick (D.-N. Dak.), a co-sponsor of the amendment, has said:

The English Language Amendment will alter very little in the lives of most Americans. Elegant French restaurants will continue to print French menus; seminarians will continue their Latin studies; Jewish youngsters will continue to attend Hebrew school; opera lovers will continue to hear their favorite works in Italian, German, or French; as before, immigrant families will meet and greet each other in their native tongue. . . . Our precious First Amendment will continue to protect free speech, as it always has and always must.

In another sense, the ELA completely would shift the direction of governmental action. Over the past two decades, responding to the heightened ethnic assertiveness of the new immigrant communities, the Federal government has promoted bilingual ballots and bilingual education, encouraged the preservation of ethnic separatism, and downplayed the importance of learning English either for full participation in the political life of the U.S. or for economic and social success here. This governmental attitude came at a time both when immigration was at a historic high and when, for the first time in American history, a majority of immigrants spoke one language other than English—Spanish.

The Government's Role

The ELA, by restating the importance of English for the unity of the U.S., would reinstate this important assumption: the government's role in the interaction of ethnic and racial groups is to assist in their integration and assimilation into public life—not to preserve and accentuate their differences. There are two key phrases in this assumption—"the government's role" and "into public life." A distinction must be made between the role of the family and voluntary organizations and the role of the government.

Just as it is not the government's role to promote or preserve any religion through public education, it is not the government's role to promote or preserve ethnic or racial distinctions or traditions. The government, through its public schools, has no business telling the descendents of Mexicans that they must learn to speak Spanish and like mariachi music, any more than it should tell the children of Italians they must speak Italian and appreciate operas, or tell the children of Jews they must learn to speak Hebrew or Yiddish and observe the holy days. If the children's parents want to preserve the languages or traditions of their homelands or people, they may do so through the family and through private schools.

Government's sphere is public life; the preservation of cultural traditions through private associations is none of its concern. Cultural, ethnic, and religious groups have no claim on the common government that would require it to assume the role of defender of their faiths or of their languages. It is this redirection, especially the possibility that the government would reverse its policy of the past two decades and begin actively to encourage the use of English in education and voting, that has aroused an active opposition to the ELA.

The rhetoric of the opponents of the English Language Amendment, especially at the local community level, is extreme both in its positive and negative claims. Robert H. Cordova, a professor of Hispanic studies at the University of Northern Colorado, in the *Houston Chronicle* (March 11, 1985), made the extravagant claim that "the present monolingual, monocultural, Anglocentric public education system must be replaced by a multilingual, multicultural, pluralistic one . . ." because the U.S. "is expected to be bilingual—Spanish and English—by the turn of the century. . . ."

If Americans still have some irrational attachment to their native language, Herman Sillas, in an article for the Hispanic Link News Service in February, 1985, assured us that "English Is Just Another Language." He wrote that, "If we as a nation want to lead the world in the future, we must recognize language for what it really is: a skill. Nothing more. . . . We need to move from the mentality of tying language to loyalty. The two are separate things."

In opposition to the ELA, Tony Salazar, a community activist in Kansas City, Mo., said in March, 1985, "I think it's wrong. I think it's racist. I think it's anti-immigration." Helen Gonzales, of the Mexican American Legal Defense and Education Fund, has said that, "It just plays into the old, anti-alien hysteria." The chairman and the executive director of the Maryland Governor's Commission on Hispanic Affairs signed a mailgram, opposing two state English-language bills, which insisted that "Underlying the motives for these bills is a prependency of prejudice and racism that is completely against the tenets of the constitution of Maryland and all laws of justice and fair play." Rick Mendoza, a spokesman for the Inland Empire Hispanic Association, called a Washington State English-language bill "clearly an act of language discrimination on equal par with racial discrimination and in direct line with Aryan Nations philosophy of one race, one religion, one language."

The Bilingual Education Argument

The intertwined anti-ELA and pro-bilingual education movements are not always, of course, so straightforward about the purpose of their cause. There is also an educational arm of the movement which insists that bilingual education is simply a tool for better education, that children whose initial language is not English learn more easily—even learn English more easily—if they are taught in their first language. The aim of bilingual education, some insist, is transition—better, fuller, speedier integration of the students into American society—not maintenance of their home countries' cultures.

There are two problems with this argument. First, there is no proof of the effectiveness of bilingual education. Impartial surveys of effectiveness studies of bilingual programs have shown that evidence for the superiority of bilingual methods is inconclusive: some bilingual programs work well for some students, some immersion or Berlitz programs work well for some students, and some English as a Second Language programs work well for some students—and some of all of them are failures. As Colorado Gov. Richard Lamm and Gary Imhoff wrote in *The Immigration Time Bomb: The Fragmenting of America,*

Bilingual programs have held sway for political, not educational, reasons. Bilingual education gives jobs and local power to members of the non-English-speaking community who work in the schools. It reinforces children's identification with members of their own ethnic group. And it preserves the distinguishing characteristics of those ethnic groups, which gives a power base to those who identify themselves as leaders of those splinter groups.

The second problem with the argument for bilingual education is that bilingual programs, represented to the public as transitional, rarely make English facility their primary objective. The political forces behind bilingual education are those which promote cultural separatism, and bilingual programs tend to become maintenance programs. Pamela S. Saur inadvertently exposed this argument in her *Spanish Today* article (July/August, 1985), "Winning the Debate on Bilingual Education":

Many advocates of bilingual education are repelled by the theory behind transitional bilingual education. They object to the negative psychological and cultural effects of a program which aims to do away with a child's own language as soon as possible, to stamp it out and replace it with English.

I personally favor maintenance and enrichment bilingual programs, continued research and continued debate on all aspects of the issue. However, I believe that, given the current conservative, budget-cutting, and xenophobic climate in this country, it is likely that all bilingual education will continue to be threatened. In such a situation, I believe that the cause of winning public acceptance for bilingual education will be advanced by spreading the information that most programs are transitional and temporary. . . .

The emotional strength of the bilingual movement, for all its excesses, lies in the sympathy it expresses with immigrants' emotional resentment against the process of assimilation. Migrants' assimilation to their new culture is a difficult and bittersweet struggle. Much of their past will be lost for the future they will gain, and they regret the loss. Those who assist in the assimilation process, those who may force it along when migrants rather would rest in an untenable position halfway between cultures, sometimes may be appreciated, but they rarely will be loved.

The people who advocate and run Americanization movements, after all, can be intolerable in their sense of superiority. They—we—are not cultural relativists. We tell immigrants that American culture and its roots in English culture may not be better than the cultures of their home countries, but that, in the U.S., they are preferable. We assert that it is better, in this country, to adopt American customs than to persist in the customs of their childhoods and to speak English, rather than the immigrants' native languages.

It is only realistic to expect that this message should be met with mixed emotions. The settlement-house "Americanizers" of the 1880's—Jane Addams, Charles Stover, and all the others— were, just like today's Americanizers, the recipients of both the gratitude and the resentment of the migrants whom they helped enter into and adjust to this society.

Irving Howe, in *World of Our Fathers*, told a wonderful story about the ambivalence new immigrants must feel toward their benefactors/tormentors. He wrote about New York's Educational Alliance, which was prominently active in immigrant programs for decades, beginning in the 1890's. The Alliance, run by German-American Jews, helped Americanize and assimilate the new Jewish immigrants from Eastern Europe. "There were morning classes for children needing preparation to enter public school; night classes for adults struggling with English; daytime classes for waiters, watchmen, and bakers who worked at night; classes in Yiddish and Hebrew; classes in cooking and sew-ing; classes in Greek and Roman history . . . ," and much more. The Alliance, with its aim of uplifting and improving its charges, advocated their immediate transformation to an American life-style, and therefore it "could never settle into harmony, either within its own institutional life or in relation to the immigrant masses. With the latter there was always distance and misunder-standing, and obtuseness of good faith."

What both the Americanizers and the immigrants knew, how-ever, for all the friction and misunderstanding between them, was that there was also this good faith. As Howe commented about the Alliance,

The German Jews, intent upon seeing that the noses of those East Side brats were wiped clean, surely proved themselves to be insufferable, and anyone raised in the clatter of Clinton Street or the denial of Cherry Street had good reason to rage against the uptown Jews. Yet, in a way, the latter were right: physical exercise and hygiene *were* essential to the well-being of the "coreligionists" and somehow, through prodding and pa-tronizing, they had to be convinced of this. The east European Jews felt free to release their bile because they knew that finally the German Jews would not abandon them, and the German Jews kept on with their good works even while reflecting on the boorishness of their "coreligionists." Out of such fiction came a modest portion of progress.

Progress for immigrants is a product of this creative friction, this tension. However, the friction and tension become serious obstacles to progress when the good faith is lost, when those who gain power or position by mediating between a dependent immigrant group and the general society are able to convince large numbers of the new immigrants that those who wish to integrate and assimilate them within the society are their enemies. In this sense, the battle between opponents and supporters of the ELA is a contest of appearances and reputations, a fight for the high ground. Sen. Symms, the chief sponsor of the ELA, summed it up in "The Nation's Language: English," *The Washington Post,* March 9, 1985:

> Unfortunately, our lavishly funded "maintenance" style bilingual education program holds students prisoners in their native language. It also ensures students a prolonged "second-class" citizenship status in America's economic mainstream.

> The ELA would be subject to the Bill of Rights and the First Amendment; it could not be used to discourage the use of foreign languages by individuals. Nor is it my intention to designate English or the Anglo-American culture as superior to any other language or culture. We merely believe that, for the American melting-pot to work, it has to have a common, unifying element.

> So, who is really xenophobic, racist, and ethnocentric? The one who, for whatever lofty reason and glib rhetoric, promotes and encourages a linguistic ghetto? Or those of us who want to "mainstream" non-English-speakers as soon as possible so they can enjoy the American dream?

ENGLISH IN A MULTICULTURAL AMERICA[2]

The protection of the Constitution extends to all—to those who speak other languages as well as to those born with English on the tongue. Perhaps it would be highly advantageous if all had ready understanding of our ordinary speech, but this cannot be coerced by methods which conflict with the Constitution—a desirable end cannot be promoted by prohibited means.

—Associate Supreme Court Justice
James Clark McReynolds
Meyer v. Nebraska, 1923

In the United States today there is a growing fear that the English language may be on its way out as the American lin-

[2]Article by Dennis Baron. From *Social Policy* 21:5–14 Spr. '91. Copyright © 1991 by Social Policy Corp. Reprinted with permission.

gua franca, that English is losing ground to Spanish, Chinese, Vietnamese, Korean, and the other languages used by newcomers to our shores.

However, while the United States has always been a multi-lingual as well as a multicultural nation, English has always been its unofficial official language. Today, a greater percentage of Americans speak English than ever before, and the descendants of nonanglophones or bilingual speakers still tend to learn English—and become monolingual English speakers—as quickly as their German, Jewish, Irish, or Italian predecessors did in the past.

Assimilated immigrants, those who after several generations no longer consider themselves "hyphenated Americans," look upon more recent waves of newcomers with suspicion. Similarly, each generation tends to see the language crisis as new in its time. But reactions to language and ethnicity are cyclical, and the new immigrants from Asia and Latin America have had essentially the same experience as their European predecessors, with similar results.

English vs. German

As early as the 18th century, British colonists in Pennsylvania, remarking that as many as one-third of the area's residents spoke German, attacked Germans in terms strikingly similar to those heard nowadays against newer immigrants. Benjamin Franklin considered the Pennsylvania Germans to be a "swarthy" racial group distinct from the English majority in the colony. In 1751 he complained,

Why should the Palatine Boors be suffered to swarm into our Settlements, and by herding together establish their Language and Manners to the exclusion of ours? Why should Pennsylvania, founded by the English, become a Colony of Aliens, who will shortly be so numerous as to Ger-manize us instead of our Anglifying them, and will never adopt our Lan-guage or Customs, any more than they can acquire our Complexion?

The Germans were accused by other 18th-century Anglos of laziness, illiteracy, clannishness, a reluctance to assimilate, exces-sive fertility, and Catholicism (although a significant number of them were Protestant). In some instances they were even blamed for the severe Pennsylvania winters.

Resistance to German, long the major minority language in the country, continued throughout the 19th century, although it was long since clear that, despite community efforts to preserve their language, young Germans were adopting English and abandoning German at a rate that should have impressed the rest of the English-speaking population.

After the US entered World War I, most states quickly banned German—and, in some extreme cases, all foreign languages—from school curricula in a wave of jingoistic patriotism. In 1918, for example, Iowa Gov. William Harding forbade the use of foreign languages in schools, on trains, in public places, and over the telephone (a more public instrument then than it is now), even going so far as to recommend that those who insisted on conducting religious services in a language other than English do so not in churches or synagogues but in the privacy of their own homes.

Similarly, in 1919 the state of Nebraska passed a broad English-only law prohibiting the use of foreign languages at public meetings and proscribing the teaching of foreign languages to any student below the ninth grade. Robert T. Meyer, a teacher in the Lutheran-run Zion Parochial School, was fined twenty-five dollars because, as the complaint read, "between the hour of 1 and 1:30 on May 25, 1920," he taught German to ten-year-old Raymond Papar, who had not yet passed the eighth grade.

Upholding Meyer's conviction, the Nebraska Supreme Court found that most parents "have never deemed it of importance to teach their children foreign languages." It agreed as well that the teaching of a foreign language was harmful to the health of the young child, whose "daily capacity for learning is comparatively small." Such an argument was consistent with the educational theory of the day, which held as late as the 1950s that bilingualism led to confusion and academic failure, and was harmful to the psychological well-being of the child. Indeed, one psychologist claimed in 1926 that the use of a foreign language in the home was a leading cause of mental retardation.

Arguing the state's brief before the U.S. Supreme Court, the Nebraska Attorney General stressed—in patriarchal terms—the enlightening power of the English language:

If it is within the police power of the state . . . to legislate respecting housing conditions in crowded cities, to prohibit dark rooms in tenement houses, to compel landlords to place windows in their tenements which will enable their tenants to enjoy the sunshine, it is within the police power of the state to compel every resident of Nebraska to so educate his children that the sunshine of American ideals will permeate the life of the future citizens of this republic. A father has no inalienable constitutional right to rear his children in physical, moral or intellectual gloom.

The US Supreme Court reversed Meyer's conviction in a land-mark decision in 1923. But the decision in *Meyer v. Nebraska* was to some extent an empty victory for language teachers: while their calling could no longer be restricted, the ranks of German classes had been devastated by the instant linguistic assimilation that World War I forced on German Americans. In 1915 close to 25 percent of the student population studied German in American high schools. Seven years later only 0.6 percent—fewer than 14,000 high school students—were taking German.

English vs. Spanish

Like German in the Midwest, Spanish was the object of vil-ification in the American Southwest. This negative attitude to-ward Spanish delayed statehood for New Mexico for over 60 years. In 1902, in one of New Mexico's many tries for statehood, a congressional subcommittee held hearings in the territory, led by Indiana Senator Albert Jeremiah Beveridge, a "progressive" Re-publican who believed in "America first: Not only America first, but America only." Witness after witness before the Beveridge subcommittee was forced to admit that in New Mexico, ballots and political speeches were either bilingual or entirely in Spanish; that census takers conducted their surveys in Spanish; that jus-tices of the peace kept records in Spanish; that the courts re-quired translators so that judges and lawyers could understand the many Hispanic witnesses; that juries deliberated in Spanish as much as in English; and that children, who might or might not learn English in schools, as required by law, "relapsed" into Span-ish on the playground, at home, and after graduation.

One committee witness suggested that the minority language situation in New Mexico resembled that in Senator Beveridge's home state of Indiana: "Spanish is taught as a side issue, as Ger-man would be in any State in the Union. . . . This younger gener-ation understands English as well as I do," And a sympathetic senator reminded his audience, "These people who speak the Spanish language are not foreigners; they are natives, are they not?"

As Franklin did the Germans in Pennsylvania, Senator Bev-eridge categorized the "Mexicans" of the American Southwest as non-natives, "unlike us in race, language, and social customs," and concluded that statehood must be contingent on assimilation. He recommended that admission to the Union be delayed until a time "when the mass of the people, or even a majority of them, shall, in the usages and employment of their daily life, have become identical in language and customs with the great body of the American people; when the immigration of English-speaking people who have been citizens of other States does its modifying work with the 'Mexican' element." Although New Mexico finally achieved its goal of statehood, and managed to write protection of Spanish into its constitution, schools throughout the Southwest forbade the use of Spanish among students. Well into the present century, children were routinely ridiculed and punished for using Spanish both in class and on the playground.

Language and Power

As the New Mexican experience suggests, the insistence on English has never been benign. The notion of a national language sometimes wears the guise of inclusion: we must all speak English to participate meaningfully in the democratic process. Sometimes it argues unity: we must speak one language to understand one another and share both culture and country. Those who insist on English often equate bilingualism with lack of patriotism. Their intention to legislate official English often masks racism and certainly fails to appreciate cultural difference: it is a thinly-veiled measure to disenfranchise anyone not like "us" (with notions of "us," the real Americans, changing over the years from those of English ancestry to northwestern European to "white" monolingual English speakers).

American culture assumes monolingual competence in English. The ability to speak another language is more generally regarded as a liability than a refinement, a curse of ethnicity and a bar to advancement rather than an economic or educational advantage.

In another response to non-English speaking American citizens, during the nineteenth century, states began instituting English literacy requirements for voting to replace older property requirements. These literacy laws generally pretended to democratize the voting process, though their hidden goal was often to prevent specific groups from voting. The first such statutes in Connecticut and Massachusetts were aimed at the Irish population of those states. Southern literacy tests instituted after the Civil War were anti-Black. California's test (1892) was aimed at Hispanics and Asians. Alaska's, in 1926, sought to disenfranchise its Native Americans. Wyoming's (1897) was anti-Finn and Washington state's (1889), anti-Chinese.

The literacy law proposed for New York State in 1915, whose surface aim was to ensure a well-informed electorate, targeted a number of the state's minorities. It was seen both as a calculated attempt to prevent New York's one million Yiddish speakers from voting and as a means of stopping the state's German Americans from furthering their nefarious war aims. When it was finally enacted in 1921, supporters of the literacy test saw it as a tool to enforce Americanization, while opponents charged the test would keep large numbers of the state's newly enfranchised immigrant women from voting. Later the law, which was not repealed until the Voting Rights Act of 1965, effectively disenfranchised New York's Puerto Rican community.

An Official Language?

Although many Americans simply assume English is the official language of the United States, it is not. Nowhere in the US Constitution is English privileged over other languages, and while a few subsequent federal laws require the use of English for special, limited purposes—air traffic control, product labels, service on federal juries—no law establishes English as the language of the land.

In the xenophobic period following World War I, several moves were made to establish English at the federal level, but none succeeded. On the other hand, many states at that time adopted some form of English-only legislation. This included regulations designating English the language of state legislatures, courts, and schools, making English a requirement for entrance into such professions as attorney, barber, physician, private detective, or undertaker, and in some states even preventing nonanglophones from obtaining hunting and fishing licenses.

More recently, official language questions have been the subject of state and local debate once again. An English Language Amendment to the U.S. Constitution (the ELA) has been before the Congress every year since 1981. In 1987, the year in which more than 74 percent of California's voters indicated their support for English as the state's official language, thirty-seven states discussed the official English issue. The next year, official language laws were passed in Colorado, Florida, and Arizona. New Mexico and Michigan have taken a stand in favor of English Plus, recommending that everyone have a knowledge of English plus another language. . . .

Official American policy has swung wildly between toleration of languages other than English and their complete eradication. But neither legal protection nor community-based efforts has been able to prevent the decline of minority languages or to slow the adoption of English, particularly among the young. Conversely, neither legislation making English the official language of a state nor the efforts of the schools has done much to enforce the use of English: Americans exhibit a high degree of linguistic anxiety but continue to resist interference with their language use on the part of legislators or teachers.

A number of states have adopted official English. Illinois, for example, in the rush of postwar isolationism and anti-British sentiment, made *American* its official language in 1923; this was quietly changed to English in 1969. Official English in Illinois has been purely symbolic; it is a statute with no teeth and no discernible range or effect. In contrast, Arizona's law, which became part of the state constitution, was the most detailed and the most restrictive of any of the sixteen state official language laws currently on the books. It required all government officials and employees—from the governor down to the municipal dog catcher—to use English and only English during the performance of government business.

[In 1990], Arizona's law was ruled unconstitutional by the US District Court for the District of Arizona. Arizona's law was challenged by Maria-Kelley Yniguez, a state insurance claims administrator fluent in Spanish and English, who had often used Spanish with clients. Yniguez feared that, since she was sworn to uphold the state constitution, speaking Spanish to clients of her agency who knew no other language might put her in legal jeopardy.

. . . Judge Paul G. Rosenblatt, of the US District Court for the District of Arizona, found that the English-only article 28 of the Arizona constitution violated the First Amendment of the US Constitution protecting free speech. The ruling voiding the Arizona law will not affect the status of other state official English laws. However, it is clear that other courts may take the Arizona decision into consideration.

Teaching Our Children

Perhaps the most sensitive area of minority-language use in the US has been in the schools. Minority-language schools have existed in North America since the 18th century. In the 19th century bilingual education was common in the Midwest—St. Louis and a number of Ohio cities had active English-German public schools—as well as in parochial schools in other areas with large nonanglophone populations. More commonly, though, the schools ignored non-English speaking children altogether, making no curricular or pedagogical concessions to their presence in class. Indeed, newly instituted classroom speech requirements in the early part of this century ensured that anglophone students with foreign accents would be sent to pathologists for corrective action. And professional licensing requirements that included speech certification tests were used to keep Chinese in California and Jews in New York out of the teaching corps.

The great American school myth has us believe that the schools Americanized generations of immigrants, giving them English and, in consequence, the ability to succeed. In fact, in allowing nonanglophone children to sink or swim, the schools ensured that most of them would fail: dropout rates for non-English speakers were extraordinarily high and English was more commonly acquired on the streets and playgrounds or on the job than in the classroom.

We tend to think past generations of immigrants succeeded at assimilation while the present generation has (for reasons liberals are willing to explain away) failed. In fact, today's Hispanics are acquiring English and assimilating in much the same way and at the same pace as Germans or Jews or Italians of earlier generations did.

California presented an extreme model for excluding children with no English: it segregated Chinese students into separate "oriental" English-only schools until well into the 20th century. The ending of segregation did little to improve the linguistic fortunes of California's Chinese-speakers, who continued to be ignored by the schools. They were eventually forced to appeal to the Supreme Court to force state authorities to provide for their educational needs. The decision that resulted in the landmark case of *Lau v. Nichols* (1974) did not, however, guarantee minority-language rights, nor did it require bilingual education, as many opponents of bilingual education commonly argue. Instead the Supreme Court ordered schools to provide education for all students whether or not they spoke English, a task our schools are still struggling to carry out.

Confusion over language in the schools seems a major factor behind official language concerns. Bilingual education is a prime

target of English-only lobbying groups, who fear it is a device for
minority language maintenance rather than for an orderly transition to English. Troubling to teachers as well is the fact that bilingual programs are often poorly defined, underfunded, and inad-
equately staffed, while parents and students frequently regard
bilingual as a euphemism for remedial. In its defense, we can say
that second language education did not come into its own in this
country until after World War II. Bilingual education, along with
other programs designed to teach English as a second language,
are really the first attempts by American schools in more than two
centuries to deal directly with the problem of non-English speaking children. They represent the first attempts to revise language
education in an effort to keep children in school; to keep them
from repeating the depressing and wasteful pattern of failure
experienced by earlier generations of immigrants and nonanglophone natives; to get them to respect rather than revile both
English, frequently perceived as the language of oppression, and
their native tongue, all too often rejected as the language of poverty and failure.

Despite resistance to bilingual education and problems with
its implementation, the theory behind it remains sound. Children
who learn reading, arithmetic, and other subjects in their native
language while they are being taught English will not be as likely
to fall behind their anglophone peers, and will have little difficulty transferring their subject-matter knowledge to English, as
their English proficiency increases. On the other hand, when
nonanglophone children or those with very limited English are
immersed in English-only classrooms and left to sink or swim, as
they were for generations, they will continue to fail at unaccept-
able rates.

English is Here to Stay

Those Americans who fear that unless English is made the official
language of the United States by means of federal and state constitutional amendments they are about to be swamped by new
waves of non-English-speakers should realize that even without
restrictive legislation, minority languages in the US have always
been marginal. Research shows that Hispanics, who now constitute the nation's largest minority-language group, are adopting
English in the second and third generation in the same way that
speakers of German, Italian, Yiddish, Russian, Polish, Chinese or
Japanese have done in the past. However, as the experience of

Hispanics in southern California suggests, simply acquiring English is not bringing the educational and economic successes promised by the melting-pot myth. Linguistic assimilation may simply not be enough to overcome more deep-seated prejudices against Hispanics.

Nonetheless, there are many minority-language speakers in the US, and with continued immigration they will continue to make their presence felt. The 1980 Census showed that one in seven Americans speaks a language other than English, or lives with someone who does. Even if the courts do not strike down English-only laws, it would be difficult to legislate minority languages out of existence because we simply have no mechanisms in this country to carry out language policy of any kind (schools, which are under local and state control, have been remarkably erratic in the area of language education). On the other hand, even in the absence of restrictive language legislation, American society enforces its own irresistible pressure to keep the United States an English-speaking nation. The Census also reports that 97 percent of Americans identify themselves as speaking English well or very well. English may not be official, but it is definitely here to stay.

If the past cycles of protective legislation for English are any indication, whatever happens in the present debate over the English Language Amendment to the US Constitution and in similar debates at the state level is likely to be minimally disruptive and only temporary. The issue of minority languages will not soon go away, and a constitutional amendment cannot force people to adopt English if they are unwilling or unable to do so. Nor will English cease to function as the nation's official language even if it does not have a constitutional amendment to establish it. . . .

LEGISLATING ASSIMILATION: THE ENGLISH-ONLY MOVEMENT[3]

Contention between people who speak different languages is as old as the story of Babel. The ancient Greeks referred to those

[3]Article by Mark R. Halton. From *The Christian Century* N 29, 1989. Copyright © 1989 Christian Century Foundation. Reprinted by permission.

who spoke in other tongues as "the babblers." Ancient Slavs called the Germans across their border "the mute" or "unspeaking" people. Today, U.S. residents whose primary language is other than English—especially Spanish speakers—are being regarded as "un-American."

A pitched battle is under way between those who consider that, for the sake of America's cohesion, English must be legislated the official language through state or federal constitutional amendments, and those who consider such attempts bigoted or xenophobic. The main goals of the English-only movement are to eliminate or limit bilingual education in the public schools; to prevent state or local governments from spending funds for translating road signs or government documents or for translators to assist non-English-speaking patients at public hospitals; and to abolish multilingual ballots—required in 375 jurisdictions by the 1965 Voting Rights Act. Florida, Colorado and Arizona—states with large Hispanic populations—voted in referendums last year to make English the official language, bringing the number of states with such laws to 17.

In contrast, New Mexico's legislature voted down an English-only law . . . and endorsed "English Plus" stating, "Proficiency on the part of our citizens in more than one language is to the economic and cultural benefit of our State and the Nation."

But what does "English only" mean? That question is being raised in California, where voters approved a language law. . . . This year [1989], a legislative committee rejected a bill that would have banned the use of languages other than English by state and local government agencies. Also, a state senate committee, responding to the U.S. Equal Employment Opportunity Commission, enacted a law prohibiting private companies from restricting their employees' use of non-English languages while at work, unless necessary for business reasons. In 1988 the Los Angeles federal appeals court, countering some companies' English-only rules, said such restrictions are not only a veiled form of discrimination but a way of increasing racism.

The groups that have led the fight "to protect English by declaring it the official language of the United States" are U.S. English (whose co-founder, S. I. Hayakawa, is a former U.S. senator from California and a retired professor of linguistics) and English First, part of the Committee to Protect the Family. These groups are on the offensive, claiming that they are trying to help non-English speakers get ahead economically and socially. U.S.

English, which claims 350,000 members, cites the "political up-heavals over language that have torn apart Canada, Belgium, Sri Lanka . . . and other nations" as a reason to ban the use of "many languages" for official purposes. . . .

Most opponents of the English-only movement—such as the Mexican-American Legal Defense Fund and the U.S. Catholic Conference's Secretariat for Hispanic Affairs—are not against ethnic groups learning English, but against the us-versus-them rhetoric advanced by many English-only advocates. George Muñoz, writing in the *Chicago Sun-Times,* has said, "Opposition to English-only is not from a desire to stay apart; most Hispanics want to integrate. But they don't want to be denied access to the mainstream while they're learning English." Muñoz argues that it's not the language of communication that should be important to the government but whether the government can make itself understood by all.

The recent English-only movement got its start in Miami—perhaps the most bilingual major city in the U.S.—in 1978, after Emmy Shafer was unable to communicate with any of the clerks at the Dade County municipal offices. They all spoke only Spanish; she, only English. Her protest led to passage of a 1980 county law stipulating that no funds could be used to translate public signs or documents into Spanish or other non-English languages.

But Miami is a special case. It contains the majority of the country's Cuban-Americans, who compose about 5 percent of the U.S. Hispanic population. They have largely avoided assimilating because they consider themselves exiles of Cuba, still awaiting the fall of the Castro government to return home. Puerto Ricans living in Miami, on the other hand, reportedly are learning English quickly, many of them vying for well-paying bilingual jobs.

On the whole, language assimilation in the U.S. has followed a four-generation pattern, according to Kenneth Wilson in *Van Winkle's Return: Change in American English, 1966–1986.* Between 1890 and 1920, for example, hundreds of thousands of Poles emigrated to the U.S. A typical Polish couple (call them the Pomykalskis) might have arrived in New York City in 1909 with an infant son and eventually settled in Chicago where they spoke only Polish at work, at mass, in the shops and, of course, at home. But in a few years their son spoke English at school, starting in first grade, while speaking Polish at home and at his after-school job. He and his Polish friends became bilingual and did not have an accent in either language.

He got married to his high school sweetheart in 1928—a Pole who had emigrated with her parents when she was 13 years old—and the two spoke English at home, she with a slight accent. With their parents they spoke Polish. Their children, the grand-children of the immigrant Pomykalskis, spoke English at home and at school, and used Polish only when speaking to Grand-mother in the kitchen. In each domain of language—school, so-cial life, work, church and family—the use of Polish diminished.

The original Pomykalskis's great-granddaughter was born in 1956 in a suburb of Columbus, Ohio. She grew up speaking no Polish and has very little connection to her Polish heritage. She is thoroughly enculturated in American ways and language. As Wil-son says, "Wistfully, this generation hopes to recover some lin-guistic access to a culture that now . . . they wish they knew bet-ter."

Some immigrants have defied assimilation. Hasidic Jews in Brooklyn speak Yiddish, and some Amish in the Midwest speak a German dialect; they have chosen to live on linguistic islands. Finnish and Scandinavian immigrants in rural communities in the northern Midwest did not quickly assimilate for geographical rea-sons. But the commercial and societal forces shaping Hispanic immigration over the past 35 years suggest a different scenario for these immigrants.

Social and economic constraints have cut off many Hispanics from mainstream American—that is, Anglo—culture. Hispanic women who work only in the home have had limited contact with U.S. culture, and language programs sponsored by local govern-ments or businesses rarely reach them. Furthermore, in many of the largest U.S. cities one finds Spanish-language radio, TV and newspapers, and videocassettes, billboards and even grocery and department store labels in Spanish—not to promote Spanish but simply to sell goods. English-only legislation would not change these realities.

But despite the social and commercial forces leading Hispan-ics away from assimilation, recent studies have concluded that first- and second-generation Hispanics have learned English as fast as Italians, Russians, Greeks, Romanians or Japanese immi-grants did at the turn of the century. An editorialist in the *Wall Street Journal* reports that an analysis of 1980 census data by pro-fessors at the Urban Institute and the University of Chicago re-veals that while a great majority of Hispanics over the age of 25 speak Spanish at home, most also speak English with proficiency.

And a study by the RAND corporation reveals that language-assimilation statistics for Hispanic immigrants are in line with the history of the Polish family discussed above. Nearly half the permanent Mexican immigrants living in California speak English well, and only about 25 percent speak Spanish exclusively. For the most part, their American-born children are bilingual and 90 percent are proficient in English. Over half of their grandchildren speak only English. David Lopez, a professor at UCLA, concludes that if immigration from Latin America dried up today (not likely to happen), language assimilation by Hispanics would be complete by the year 2030. Leonard Dinnerstein and David M. Reimers in *Ethnic Americans: A History of Immigration and Assimilation* believe that "with so much more public assistance available than had been given to immigrants in previous generations, it is possible that the newcomers may not need as long a time to move into the mainstream of American society."

The issue that most divides the English-only advocates and their opponents is bilingual education. Former President Reagan spoke against it. Congress has debated it. Newspaper op-ed pages and radio talk shows have discussed it. "Bilingual education" is really a misnomer, since the goal of such programs is not to produce bilingual students, but to make Hispanic, Chinese or Vietnamese students proficient in English while drawing on their own native language as a transitional tool. U.S. English and other groups claim that bilingual education helps perpetuate adherence to non-English tongues. But the National Association for Bilingual Education points to research revealing the advantages of bilingual education: when students participate for an average of two to three years researchers notice "improved academic achievement test scores, reduced rates of school dropout and student absenteeism, increased community involvement in education, and enhanced student self-esteem."

Many older people who emigrated to the U.S. when they were in grade school were thrown into English-only classrooms and made to swim or sink. They claim that all their immigrant peers learned to swim, and quickly. However, no studies were done at the time to determine how many immigrant children sank— dropping out of school or never living up to their potential. Language acquisition can be a slow arduous process for many. And there is more to education than learning a language. Learning math, science, music or art in one's native language gives a student skills readily transferable to the English-speaking world. A student does not need to relearn the subjects taught in Spanish when later reviewing them in English.

Though the U.S. has never had an official policy of introducing English to immigrants, language assimilation has always been startlingly rapid. Kenji Hakuta in *Mirror of Language: The Debate on Bilingualism* credits economic interests and "benign neglect" of one's own language as the leading causes of immigrants' forsaking their mother tongues. Another reason cited is that educational psychologists urged immigrant parents to avoid speaking a non-English language at home on the false premise that bilingualism stunts the academic growth of children. While no linguists tout this theory today, many proponents of the English-only movement still believe that there is room for but one language in a young person's mind.

When immigrants poured into America in the 19th century one of three scenarios could have played out. American culture could have transformed the immigrants (Americanization or assimilation); the culture could have been transformed by the immigrants (melting pot); or the culture could have split into separatist groups. For over 150 years the pattern has been one of assimilation, "a move," Dinnerstein and Reimers write, "into the mainstream of American life [requiring] the relinquishment of cherished cultural ties." Immigrants start in separate groups—as Hispanics do today by attending Spanish language churches and marrying other Hispanics—but within four generations they assimilate, no longer calling themselves, for example, Polish-Americans but simply Americans.

Political unity, communication and transportation systems and financial factors will keep the U.S. an English-speaking nation. English does not need to be legislated the official language; gentler forces than those proposed by English-only proponents will produce that end. As the U.S. enters the '90s, a new awareness of other cultures' music, language, customs, food, electronic goods and even political ways is transforming our life. There is a growing realization that Americans of northern European descent have much to learn from U.S. residents of Latin American or Asian backgrounds. Perhaps in the 21st century the strict assimilation patterns of the past will yield to more "melting"—the mixing of cultures in a way that changes the flavor of the entire society.

WORKPLACE LANGUAGE RULES[4]

Some employers impose restrictions against the use of a language other than English in their workplaces. Reasons given for the restrictions include: The use of a foreign language in a workplace is inappropriate; English has been made the official language of their state and safety and public relations require that only English be spoken.

Can employers lawfully regulate language in the workplace? It is largely an unsettled issue. There are only a few court decisions on the matter. Guidelines issued by the Equal Employment Opportunity Commission (EEOC) indicate that prohibiting employees from speaking a language other than English amounts to national origin bias under the Civil Rights Act. However, the guidelines permit language restrictions if they constitute a "business necessity." It should be noted that EEOC guidelines do not have the force of law but courts look to them for direction.

A case that followed EEOC guidelines held that a California meat packing company's requirement that employees speak only English on the plant floor violated the Civil Rights Act. Up to 60 percent of the company's employees spoke Spanish and English fluency was not required for hiring. But management issued an English-only requirement, maintaining the rule was necessary to avoid friction among employees, improve plant safety and increase productivity. The EEOC found that the company discriminated on the basis of national origin and retaliated against Spanish-speaking employees by establishing the rule.

A federal district court agreed with the EEOC, saying that there were less restrictive alternatives available to increase employee productivity and discipline. The court observed that a 1986 amendment to the California constitution declaring that English is the state's official language may have raised "employer consciousness" to the English-only rules and "emboldened them, improperly, to take those risks." It also observed that the state legislature did not pass any law to enforce the constitutional amendment. (Garcia vs. Spun Steak Co., DC, N. Calif., N. C91-1949RHS)

[4]Article by William E. Lissy, staffwriter. From *Supervision* 54:20–21 Apr '93. Reprinted by permission of © National Research Bureau.

Interestingly, another meat packing company in California is not uncomfortable with different languages being spoken in the workplace. At Clougherty Packing Co. in Los Angeles, it is not uncommon for bilingual supervisors to manage employees in their native language and employees are not required to have a knowledge of English.

"Restrictions against the use of a language other than English in the workplace have become very prevalent," says Kathryn Imahara, director of the Asian Pacific American Legal Center's Language Rights Project in Southern California, which provides legal services and civil rights support to immigrants from Asia and the Pacific Islands. Acknowledging that English-only rules may be necessary in certain situations—a hospital operating room or work involving dangerous equipment, for example—Imahara contends that "bans against using a second language are oppressive and affect workers' fundamental civil rights."

CLOSING THE WORKPLACE LANGUAGE GAP[5]

Schools have no monopoly on language instruction. As increasing numbers of adult immigrants join the U.S. labor force, employers are setting up their own programs to help them hone their English skills. Most of the programs use the English-as-a-second-language (ESL) approach, in which the instructor speaks English almost exclusively. The primary goal is to improve communication between English-speaking managers and foreign-language-speaking workers, most of them Spanish-speaking. The programs also help foreign-language speakers communicate with their English-speaking co-workers.

Tru Lingua Inc., puts a new twist on some of the workplace language programs it offers to corporate clients. While the Santa Ana, Calif., firm has been offering typical vocational ESL programs for nearly 10 years, it also teaches foreign languages to English-speaking executives. "With all the foreign business take-

[5]Article from *CQ Researcher* 3:714 Ag '93. Copyright © 1993 by CQ Researcher. Reprinted with permission.

overs that have been occurring in this country," says June Fenner, Tru Lingua's project manager, "we're finding companies where suddenly all the top executives speak Italian, or German, or Japanese. And they want the second echelon [of management] to learn their language."

As with schoolchildren, the amount of time an adult needs to learn a second language varies from individual to individual. "We've found that many Hispanic workers had very little schooling in Spanish," says Fenner, "so we sometimes have to start at how to read and write, and learning the alphabet. In a situation like that, we would like the student worker to have at least 200 training hours."

But if the worker had even an elementary education in Spanish, "then within 100 or 150 hours he can generally learn enough English to meet the demands of the workplace." The better-educated workers learn English faster, Fenner says, because, "If you can read and write in one language, you have grasped concepts that make it much easier to acquire another language."

Tru Lingua strives to teach workers enough to "attend department meetings conducted in English, read engineering change orders or fill out inventory reports. In some cases, we've seen workers who attended our programs go on to sophisticated training in subjects like statistical process control."

Tru Lingua's ESL programs are tailored to the specific needs of the client company. "If it's a furniture business, the workers need to learn furniture terminology in English," says Fenner. "If the company makes circuit boards, the workers need to know that terminology. Schools take a much broader approach."

Some school systems, indeed, have branched out into business-oriented language instruction themselves. Last year, for example, some 330 employees from 13 companies participated in the English in the Workplace adult-education program of the Fairfax County, Va., public schools. Some companies sign up just once or twice, while others remain clients year after year.

Participants in the Fairfax program represent many different nationalities and language groups. Of the First American Bank employees enrolled in a recent Fairfax ESL program, says Robin Schrage, the program's coordinator, 30 percent spoke East Asian mainland languages such as Korean, Vietnamese and Cambodian; 21 percent, Spanish; 16 percent, various Indian languages; 13 percent, Farsi; 9 percent, Tagalog; and 7 percent spoke various African languages.

Regardless of their native tongue, all participants in the Fairfax program attend the same classes. "The common language [of instruction] is English," says Schrage.

Supporters of workplace literacy say it can save businesses from potentially costly mistakes by employees with shaky English—the hospital employee who enters the wrong data on a patient's chart, for example, or the factory worker who can't read posted safety instructions.

Such avoidable mishaps can lead to crippling financial setbacks, notes John O'Malley, director of the Los Angeles Unified School District's Working Smart workplace language program. "The bottom line . . . is that businesses will suffer huge losses in production, efficiency and, perhaps, lawsuits because there were communication breakdowns within the workplace."

IV. EDUCATION AND OFFICIAL ENGLISH

EDITOR'S INTRODUCTION

One of the most frequent reasons given for establishing English as the official language is the need to counter the use of bilingual education programs with minorities, particularly Hispanics and Asians. It is argued that the main effect of bilingual programs is to assist these populations in their wish to remain separate rather than assimilate in mainstream America. Supporters of bilingual education, citing research that says an average of six to eight years is required to compete academically in a second language, hold that use of the student's native language demonstrates its value, encourages student self-esteem, and assists in the eventual transition to English.

A recent issue of *CQ Researcher*, devoted to the subject of bilingual education, provides the context for this section, tracing the history of bilingualism and bilingual education and discussing the passage of the Bilingual Education Act in 1968 and other important legal decisions.

In the second article Mary McGroarty, writing in *Educational Researcher*, describes the current debate over bilingual education. She contends that the three main influences being brought to bear on bilingual education by society are the legacy of the civil rights movement, the competition for jobs, and the increased immigration from Asia and Latin America. The conflict is further fueled by shrinking state and federal monies to support bilingual education and the growing recognition that bilingual education has merit.

As the first of a three-part series on bilingual education appearing in the *Phoenix* [Az] *Gazette*, Lisa Davis's article describes one of the most successful bilingual programs in the United States and chronicles the mix of factors contributing to the success of the Calexico, California program. These include a willingness to experiment, an understanding by teachers of the student situation, a recognition of the expense of acquiring and retaining good teachers, and an aggressive program to acquire funding.

The majority of bilingual education and English-as-a-second-language (ESL) programs takes place within the elementary school. However, with the influx of foreign students, this need has flowed into higher education. Dr. Judith W. Rosenthal, in *The Chronicle of Higher Education,* describes the frustration of colleges and universities unprepared to meet this need, especially in the field of science. She suggests several language programs that can be considered by institutions willing to address this deficiency.

The next article, "'The Babel Myth': The English-Only Movement and Its Implications for Libraries" by Ingrid Betancourt, focuses on the responsibilities of public libraries to meet the needs of all people within the community regardless of ethnic, cultural, or linguistic background.

The final article, a statement by Albert Shanker, President of the American Federation of Teachers, contends that twenty years after the Supreme Court decision that gave rise to bilingual education, the regulations governing the programs may in fact be hindering the original goals.

BILINGUAL EDUCATION[1]

Early Programs

Today's debate over bilingual education was spawned, ultimately, by the old controversy about what it means to be an American. Since the early days of the republic, a philosophical gulf has divided cultural assimilationists and pluralists. Assimilationists believe the mission of U.S. schools is to nurture a common language—English—and a common national identity. Pluralists feel diverse languages and customs enrich the U.S. cultural stew and should be allowed to flourish.

Despite the philosophical differences, non-English and bilingual education programs were not uncommon in 18th- and 19th-century America. Before the Civil War, for example, some Cincinnati schools taught in both English and German. "These

[1]Article from *CQ Researcher* 3:704–712 Ag 13 '93. Copyright © 1992 by CQ Researcher. Reprinted with permission.

institutions spent half the day on German-language instruction and half a day on everything else, including English-language instruction," wrote Professor Joel Perlmann of the Harvard Graduate School of Education. "The German half of the day was apparently limited to instruction in the language itself, rather than being used for the teaching of other subjects in that language."

German-English schools also were started during the period in Indianapolis, St. Louis, Baltimore and other cities with large German communities. Additionally, there were French-English programs in Louisiana, Spanish-English programs in the Territory of New Mexico and scattered Norwegian, Czech, Italian, Polish and Dutch programs.

In fact, some Native Americans were among the nations' bilingual pacesetters. "The Cherokees established and operated an educational system of 21 schools and two academies, which enrolled 1,100 pupils and produced a population 90 percent literate in its native language," educator Diego Castellanos wrote. "They used bilingual materials to such an extent that by 1852 Oklahoma Cherokees had a higher English literacy level than the white populations of either Texas or Arkansas."

Impact of Nationalism

Many bilingual schools perished, however, in the wave of anti-Catholicism and xenophobia that swept the nation in the late 1800s and early 1900s. Most educators at the time embraced the melting-pot theory and, not surprisingly, advocated English-only instruction. Ellwood P. Cubberly, a well-known educational historian, characterized the country's new immigrants as "illiterate, docile, lacking in self-reliance and initiative and not possessing the Anglo-Teutonic conceptions of law, order and government." The role of the schools, in Cubberly's view, was "to assimilate and amalgamate these people as a part of the American race."

President Theodore Roosevelt was one of the country's foremost advocates of "Americanization," as the assimilationist doctrine was called. "There is no room in this country for hyphenated Americanism." Roosevelt wrote in *The Foes of Our Household* (published in 1917, eight years after he left the White House). "[A]ny man who comes here . . . must adopt the language which is now the native tongue of our people. . . . It would not be merely a misfortune, but a crime to perpetuate differences of language in this country."

Every immigrant, said Roosevelt, should be given the opportunity to learn English in day school or night school—"and if, after say five years, he has not learned English, he should be sent back to the land from whence he came."

U.S. entry into World War I brought anti-German feeling to a boil and delivered the coup de grâce to what remained of bilingual education in the United States. The surviving foreign-language schools, most of them German, were forced to shut down by laws either mandating English-only instruction or reserving public education funds for English-only schools. By 1923, 34 of the 48 states had adopted English-only policies.

The resurgence of nationalism also found expression in the restrictive immigration law enacted by Congress in 1924. The measure established a two-phase quota formula. During the interim phase, the annual number of immigrants from each European country was limited to no more than 2 percent of the total of foreign-born persons of that nationality living in the United States at the time the 1890 census was taken. In the second phase, which took effect in 1929, an overall quota of 150,000 was apportioned among the various European countries in the same proportion that immigrants from those nations were represented in the U.S. population.

The national-origins system initially required little change in the low quotas assigned to countries of Southern and Eastern Europe. But it entailed substantial reductions in the German, Irish and Scandinavian quotas and a large increase for the British. Britain's 66,000 quota far exceeded Germany's 26,000 limit, the next largest. But Britain never fulfilled its quota, so the net effect was to cut actual immigration far below the volume authorized by the law. Another effect was to further entrench the English language and Anglo-Saxon culture in American life.

Around this time, a U.S. Supreme Court endorsement of foreign-language instruction seemed to buck the trend toward nationalism, if somewhat gently. Ruling in *Meyer v. Nebraska*, the court held in 1923 that a Nebraska law barring the teaching of foreign languages to elementary school children was unconstitutional. Proficiency in a foreign language, it declared, was "not injurious to the health, morals or understanding of the ordinary child."

However, the court said, the power of a state to "make reasonable regulations for all schools, including a requirement that they shall give instruction in English, is not questioned." It also noted,

"The desire of the Legislature to foster a homogeneous people with American ideals, prepared readily to understand current discussions of civic matters, is easy to appreciate."

After the *Meyer* decision, two educators observed, "the strict English-only instruction laws were generally either repealed or ignored." Declining immigration may also have slowed the Americanization movement. Between 1921 and 1930, 4.1 million immigrants entered the country—less than half the 1901–1910 total. Between 1931 and 1940, moreover, only 528,431 newcomers arrived—fewer than in any decade since the 1820s.

Bilingual Revival

For the next 20 years, until the 1960s, interest in bilingual schooling was limited. Then it blossomed, spurred initially by the arrival in south Florida of thousands of Cuban refugees after Fidel Castro came to power in 1959. To help arriving children adjust to their new country, Dade County (Miami) in 1963 began an experimental bilingual education program in the first three grades of the Coral Way Elementary School. Both Spanish- and English-speaking children participated, since the program's goal was to foster bilingualism among native speakers of both tongues.

The Coral Way experiment was deemed a success, prompting educators to look for explanations. Josué M. González cited several factors, including the fact that many refugee families came from the professional classes and thus "were able to offer the services of trained teachers and other educational personnel from their own ranks." And since "most of the early Cuban refugees were of predominantly European stock, racism was not a significant factor."

Other communities, primarily in the Southwest, soon adopted variations of the Coral Way model, among them Laredo and San Antonio, Texas. By 1969, some 56 bilingual programs were under way; all were Spanish-English except for a Navajo-English project at Rough Rock, Ariz.

Congressional Support. The widespread support for bilingual education helped advocates persuade lawmakers to fund bilingual programs during congressional hearings in 1967. Legislation approving funding cleared Congress in December 1967 and was signed by President Lyndon B. Johnson on Jan. 2, 1968.

The Bilingual Education Act, adopted as Title VII of the reauthorized Elementary and Secondary Education Act, made bilingual instruction more appealing to school districts across the country. The availability of federal money helped the program directly, while favorable public opinion provided an indirect boost. The 1968 law did not require local school districts to establish bilingual programs, but it encouraged their development by offering grants.

Early programs funded under the law revealed a greater need for bilingual education than had been anticipated. Accordingly, Congress revised Title VII when ESEA came up for reauthorization again in 1974. The 1974 act broadened and clarified the federal role in bilingual education. For the first time, federal money was made available for training teachers and developing curricula and instructional materials.

Supreme Court's 1974 Ruling. In a related 1974 development, the Supreme Court ruled in *Lau v. Nichols* that the San Francisco school system discriminated against some 1,800 Chinese American students by failing to help them overcome their language handicap, thereby denying them "a meaningful opportunity to participate in the public educational program." The school district's failure to take positive action to help students who were not fluent in English, the court said, violated Section 601 of the 1964 Civil Rights Act, which bans discrimination "on the ground of race, color or national origin" in programs receiving federal financial assistance.

There was some confusion at first as to what *Lau* meant. The court did not order the San Francisco school system to set up a bilingual program. In fact, it did not specify any remedy. "Teaching English to the students of Chinese ancestry who do not speak the language is one choice," the justices declared. "Giving instructions to the group in Chinese is another. There may be others." What solution would be adopted was left up to the lower court and the school district to work out.

However, a task force appointed by the U.S. Office of Civil Rights to study ways of enforcing the Supreme Court's decision issued a report in August 1975 that seemed to indicate that bilingual programs were indeed being mandated. The report prompted some regional directors of the U.S. Department of Health, Education and Welfare to tell local school districts to establish bilingual programs.

The ensuing furor prompted the Office of Civil Rights to issue a memo on April 8, 1976, explaining that the so-called "*Lau* remedies" were "guidelines only." But the memo added that the burden of proving the acceptability of alternative remedies rested upon the school districts involved.

Immigration Reform. By this time, bilingual education was coming under closer scrutiny because of massive increases in the number of non-English-speaking children in the country. Much of the rise stemmed from 1965 immigration reforms, which abolished the 1920s-era national-origin quota system. The 1965 law substituted an overall annual ceiling of 170,000 immigrants from the Eastern Hemisphere, with no more than 20,000 to come from any one country. The Western Hemisphere's ceiling was set at 120,000.

These provisions brought dramatic changes in the racial and ethnic composition of immigration. With Europeans no longer receiving preference, formerly overlooked nationality groups seized their chance to become U.S. citizens. By the late 1970s, Latin Americans made up 42 percent of total immigrants, while Europeans dropped to 13 percent (from 68 percent in the 1950s).

Immigration from Asia also zoomed. According to the U.S. Immigration and Naturalization Service, only 445,300 Asian immigrants came to the United States between 1961 and 1970. The total then rose to 1.6 million between 1971 and 1980 and to 2.8 million between 1981 and 1990. Legislation making it easier for refugees to gain permanent residence in the United States helped swell the post-1970 influx from Asia.

Reagan-Era Changes

These developments fueled demands for language training tailored to the needs of immigrant children with little or no knowledge of English. In 1980, under a proposal backed by President Jimmy Carter, English-language instruction became mandatory for schools with at least 20 children from the same language-minority group. But President Ronald Reagan, who viewed education as fundamentally a local, not federal, responsibility, rescinded the regulation in 1981, shortly after taking office.

That same year, the Reagan administration began pressing Congress to drop any regulations requiring bilingual-grant recipients to provide native-language instruction. In 1984, Congress approved a major overhaul of federal aid to bilingual education as part of an omnibus bill to extend 10 expiring education programs. Under a compromise worked out by the House Education and Labor Committee, a portion of the money appropriated for bilingual grants was earmarked for alternatives to transitional bilingual instruction. The portion set aside was to range from 4 percent to 10 percent, depending on whether Congress increased spending for bilingual aid.

Administration officials, meanwhile, maintained a verbal barrage against bilingual education, pounding home the message that the program was ineffective. The government's chief spokesman on the issue was National Endowment for the Humanities Chairman William J. Bennett, who became secretary of Education in January 1985. In a speech that September, Bennett labeled the Bilingual Education Act of 1968 a "failure." He added, "After 17 years of federal involvement, and after $1.7 billion of federal funding, we have no evidence that the children whom we sought to help . . . have benefited."

On another occasion, Bennett declared that "the overriding purpose of bilingual education must be to enable children to become fluent in English as quickly as possible." He also blamed the program for failing to prevent Hispanic students from dropping out of school and for their low academic achievement.

Several private groups established in the 1980s share Bennett's views on the primacy of English. U.S. English, founded in 1983 by former U.S. Sen. S. I. Hayakawa, R-Calif., takes the position that "a shared language provides a cultural guidepost that we must maintain for the sake of our country's unity, prosperity and democracy." English First, founded in 1986, has said it will campaign for a constitutional amendment to make English the "official language" of the United States. And Learning English Advocates Drive (LEAD), founded in 1987, proposed renaming the Bilingual Education Act as the English Language Development Act and changing the limited-English-proficiency designation (LEP) to English learner (EL).

When the Bilingual Education Act again came up for reauthorization in 1988, the Reagan administration called for removal of all restrictions on English-only, alternative-instruction programs. Congress declined to go that far, but it did agree to allocate up to 25 percent of bilingual-instruction funding for alternative approaches, such as English as a second language and English immersion. The legislation also prohibited students, except in certain cases, from participating in a federally funded bilingual education program for more than three years. Moreover, it established within the Department of Education an Office of Bilingual Education and Minority Language Affairs (OBEMLA) to oversee bilingual education programs.

During the 1988 election campaign, Republican presidential nominee George Bush announced that he intended to build a record as "the education president." However, Bush showed little interest in bilingual programs after taking office, at least to some extent because the ESEA did not come up for reauthorization during his term. The main item on his education agenda was "America 2000," a comprehensive reform program that stressed school-choice plans.

Cautious Optimism

While educators, politicians and parents debated bilingual education throughout the 1980s, the number of LEP children was steadily growing. According to 1990 U.S. Census data, 13.9 percent of all children ages 5 to 17—nearly one of every seven schoolchildren—spoke a language other than English at home. Between 1980 and 1990, moreover, the population of school-age children who usually speak a language other than English rose by 41.2 percent, compared with a 4 percent decline in the total number of schoolchildren nationwide over the same period.

The Stanford Working Group says there are from 2.3 million to 3.5 million LEP students, and that federally funded bilingual education programs "touch only a small proportion" of them. The group cites a recent Education Department study that found 810,000 LEP students participate in Chapter 1 programs for the disadvantaged. According to the same study, Title VII programs served about 310,000 students in fiscal 1991—or between 9 and 13 percent of the total LEP population.

The federal bilingual education programs that do exist often are hard-pressed for funds. Congress appropriated $196 million for Title VII in the current fiscal year, the Stanford Working Group noted—a sum 33 percent lower than the fiscal 1981 appropriation after taking inflation into account. "And this decrease in funding occurred during a period when the number of LEP students increased significantly."

Hope for Reauthorization. After the funding cuts of the past 12 years, bilingual education advocates see this year's [1993] effort to reauthorize the Elementary and Secondary Education Act as an opportunity to regain lost momentum. Though the Clinton administration has yet to propose draft legislation, it is perceived as more sympathetic toward bilingual education than the Reagan and Bush administrations were. The recent appointment of Eugene E. García as director of OBEMLA seemed to confirm this appraisal. García, a professor of education and psychology at the University of California-Santa Cruz, is a member of the Stanford Working Group.

Education Secretary Richard W. Riley also has reassured supporters of bilingualism. In February, [1993] for instance, he said that "the bilingual nature of our country is a plus, not a minus, and I don't think the school system should lend itself to one or the other, but teach all cultures."

Riley added further backing to the bilingualists in May, [1993] suggesting that Chapter 1 funds be funneled to the poorest school districts. To win votes for the program in 1965, President Johnson wanted legislation that would reach as many school districts in as many congressional districts as possible. But now, said Riley, "I do think we need to do a better job of targeting those funds and not spreading them so thin that for a poor area they have a lot less impact than they should."

Echoing Riley, the working group has proposed rewriting the Chapter 1 funding formula to deliver more aid to high-poverty schools. At the same time, the group would make it easier for the most disadvantaged LEP students to qualify for Chapter 1 programs. To this end, it would repeal the provision requiring participants to "have needs stemming from educational deprivation and not related solely to limited English proficiency." To make sure they are in compliance with this rule, some school districts routinely exclude students from Chapter 1 programs until they are proficient in English.

New Initiatives

For its part, the National Association for Bilingual Education has concentrated on rewriting Title VII. Among other things, NABE's draft bill calls for substantially higher funding levels—beginning at $300 million in fiscal 1994, which starts Oct. 1, and rising to $550 million in fiscal 1997. The group also favors promoting the director of OBEMLA to assistant secretary of Education, a move also recommended by the working group.

NABE's main objective, however, is to refocus Title VII. Charging that the bilingual program dissipates money and energy by supporting too many diverse instructional modes, NABE wants the program to take a more focused, systemwide approach. The emphasis would shift to program coordination for the purpose of holding LEP students to high academic standards. Achievement in non-language subjects would be stressed along with proficiency in English and a second language. And improved teacher training and parental involvement would be encouraged as well.

The Stanford Working Group also examined Title VII, suggesting that the 25-year-old program's "lighthouse" role in policy-making be strengthened. According to Chairman Kenji Hakuta, a Stanford University education professor, the group "want[s] to call attention to the fact that there really is no government office in the United States that deals with language policy issues." He added, "One model we might consider is Australia, which has a national language policy office that deals with immigrant and aboriginal languages. Our nearest equivalent to that is OB-EMLA."

Foes Seek Changes. Foes of bilingualism, meanwhile, are pressing for such laws as the proposed Language of Government Act of 1993 supported by U.S. English, which would make English the federal government's official language. (The legislation would expressly permit use of other languages in areas such as public health, safety, information, judicial proceedings and education.)

A bill introduced by Rep. Roth would go further. His Declaration of Official Language Act would not only make English the nation's official language but also end "failed bilingual education programs." Says P. George Tryfiates, executive director of English First, "Bilingual education has failed at the one thing Congress has asked it to do: Teach children English."

Another bill supported by U.S. English would give employers tax credits for the cost of providing English-language instruction to employees, both newly arrived immigrants and poorly educated native-born Americans. Such workplace-based programs are seen as benefiting the entire economy by opening paths to better jobs and boosting productivity. Similar legislation introduced by Congress last year was backed by the NABE, which seldom agrees with U.S. English.

NABE Executive Director Lyons explained that workplace literacy programs further his organization's aim of "assisting families as educational units." That means NABE's sphere of interest extends beyond school-age children to embrace their parents, too. Older family members may enroll in adult-education programs, "some of which are tied to the workplace."

California's Plight

As lawmakers in Washington argue about bilingual education, most of the action in the field continues to take place at the state and local levels. Recent developments in California, a national pacesetter in bilingual instruction, have yielded both gains and setbacks.

Bilingual education's status in California has been somewhat uncertain since 1987, when the state's basic law on the subject was allowed to lapse. A bill approved last year by the Legislature would have required schools with 100 or more students who speak the same primary language other than English to offer at least one of three types of bilingual instruction. However, Republican Gov. Pete Wilson vetoed the measure, saying the state could not afford it.

A July 9 [1993] report by California's Little Hoover Commission, a state government watchdog group, also troubled bilingualism advocates. The commission charged that requiring students to be taught core courses in their native tongue until they knew English was "divisive, wasteful and unproductive." Despite a near-doubling of the number of non-English-speaking students since 1987, the commission said, the number of those who become fluent in English has remained stuck in the 60,000-a-year range for a decade. This, in turn, "indicates that either thousands of children are not making progress in English or assessments are not being done properly."

State Department of Education officials immediately assailed the report's conclusions. Norman Gold, head of the department's bilingual education unit, said he was appalled that the commission "would be so careless" and insisted it had misrepresented state policy.

To at least some degree, the commission's fault-finding is counterbalanced by the bilingual-education success stories reported by individual school districts. In Calexico, Calif., for example, on the Mexican border, 95 miles east of San Diego, the dropout rate among Hispanic students is less than half the statewide average. School administrators attribute the achievement to a systemwide approach to teaching Hispanic LEP students, who account for about 80 percent of Calexico's school enrollment.

"We don't even think that much in terms of bilingual education anymore," said Superintendent Roberto Moreno. "We just have the basic programs, and in some of the basic programs, Spanish is the vehicle for instruction."

The Calexico experience accords with Kenji Hakuta's view that the United States is "light-years ahead" of other countries in providing bilingual education. That includes Canada and Australia, he says, "the two other primarily immigrant countries." Title VII "let a lot of innovations get tried," Hakuta adds, and "some of them have really done well." The point of the Stanford Working Group report "was to say, 'Let's use that information.' OBEMLA possibly stands ready to do that."

THE SOCIETAL CONTEXT OF BILINGUAL EDUCATION[2]

The intensity of debate that surrounds bilingual education reflects strongly held value positions and tensions that frequently have little to do with curricular or pedagogical questions regarding optimal educational programs for students who do not know English. These value positions are realized in pressures brought to bear on educational actors and agencies by parents, teachers, administrators, school board members, and legislators, who reflect and articulate language issues from their own particular perspectives, including the need for academic achievement, the need to learn English and assimilate to a mainstream way of life, and the value of other languages and cultures.

While a survey of the many social influences shaping the context of current bilingual education programs is well beyond the scope of this paper, three factors should be briefly noted. First come the demographic changes in many school districts brought about by the increased immigration from Asia and Latin America allowed by the immigration reforms of 1965. Second is the changing labor market, which makes completion of formal schooling ever more important as competition for jobs becomes keener and the rate of job growth decreases. Finally comes the legacy of the civil rights movement of the 1960s: the institutional recognition of the legitimate demands of minority groups to have a voice in the curriculum, teaching methods, and materials used to educate their children. Proponents of bilingual education hold that use of

[2]Article by Mary McGroarty. From *Educational Researcher* 21:7–9, 24 Mr. '92. Copyright © 1992 by American Educational Research Association. Reprinted with permission.

the native language in instruction demonstrates the legitimacy of the language, acknowledges the power of the community whose language is used, and gives students heightened self-esteem, besides improving chances for academic success.

Background of Current Policy Initiatives

Historically, Americans have viewed language use as a matter to be settled pragmatically rather than ideologically. Heath (1988) notes that individual language choice in the United States has always rested on "good faith," the implied trust in the individual citizen to select the form of expression best suited to accomplish the goals at hand. The Constitution makes no reference to choice of a national language; when debates have arisen about linguistic unity as a prerequisite of national unity, they have reflected political, social, and economic issues, never purely linguistic ones (Heath, 1981, p. 8). Constitutional protections of free speech have included the freedom to choose the language one will use as well as the content one will discuss, establishing a "tolerance-oriented" tradition of language rights (Baron, 1990; Kloss, 1977).

The current federal legal mandate for bilingual education in the United States rests on the Supreme Court's 1974 *Lau v. Nichols* decision, which found that treating all children "equally" by putting them in English-speaking classrooms even if they spoke no English did not provide them with equal access to education, a decision reflecting the value position that the language of instruction is simply a means to achieving equal rights to education. Remedies were left to local discretion, with bilingual education and English-as-a-second-language instruction as two options and with the Court recognizing that other options may have also existed. Related federal regulations promoted bilingual education as the option of choice where there were large numbers of elementary school children from the same language background who did not know English. Thus bilingual instruction was presented as one way to achieve the larger goal of equal opportunity in education, a core value in public debates since the civil rights era.

The suggested remedy of using the native language in instruction was controversial from the beginning, not only because of shortages of trained teachers and materials (which persist up to the present in most cases, to a greater degree in some languages than in others) but also because the compliance mechanisms associated with federal funds in this area gave the federal government new power in influencing local education. Education, a responsibility long reserved for the states, was now subject to greater federal oversight; this represented a change from past forms of governance affecting non-English-speaking students in the United States. Though not the only initiative of the 1970s to signal a new federal role, bilingual education met resistance for structural as well as substantive reasons from the beginning. Nevertheless, some successful bilingual projects, marked by a pattern of mutual accommodation as federal mandates were worked out according to local circumstance, became established (Sumner & Zellman, 1977).

During the 1980s, though, both federal policy leadership and funding declined. Real spending related to the Bilingual Education Act dropped 47% while support for all educational programs dropped 8% (Lyons, 1990, p. 74), even as numbers of potentially eligible students grew, particularly in urban school districts and in the sunbelt. Thus the pedagogical and fiscal leadership within the federal agencies concerned with bilingual education eroded, leaving local educational authorities with larger eligible populations but a shrinking base of federal support for special language services. At the same time, the more conservative social agenda of the 1980s led to demands for local flexibility fueled by ideological trends as well as funding shortages.

Furthermore, concerns about standards of English usage and literacy for all students surfaced again during the 1980s with the publication of several reports (e.g., National Commission on Excellence in Education, 1983) suggesting an ominous decline in educational standards. Such perceptions helped to create a mentality directing educational efforts away from equity and toward the pursuit of academic excellence, defined and assessed in English.

The educational value of other languages was not denigrated entirely; it was instead redefined as part of the overall program of academic rigor prescribed to counteract the perceived slackness of the curriculum. The educational crisis reports implied that as long as the study of other languages supplemented a demanding curriculum taught in English, it would be a benefit, especially to the college-bound. The reports rarely acknowledged that second-language instruction could conserve and develop the linguistic abilities of students who already spoke another native language, nor did they address the difficulties of urging widespread

foreign-language instruction in a society in which most adults
found few uses for a second language in their daily lives.

English Only vs. English Plus: Unum or E Pluribus?

The official English movement, which gathered momentum
in the early 1980s, is behind the legislation now passed in 17 states
to make English the official state language through constitutional amendments or special statutes (Piatt, 1990). Some of these
laws might be called mainly ceremonial in intent; others, like
California's Proposition 63, are actively intended to outlaw the
use of other languages, for they give individual parties the right
to sue to enforce the statute (Dyste, 1989). Tensions between
English-only supporters and opponents demonstrate that each
has coalesced around one part of the motto on American coins:
English-only supporters perceive linguistic diversity as harmful to
national unity, emphasizing the *unum;* English-only opponents
define language regulation and restriction as anathema to individual liberty, emphasizing the *e pluribus* origins of American national union.

The English-only movement represents not the official stance
of any elected government body in the United States but a coalition of private lobbying groups with a strong nativist strain
(Crawford, 1989, pp. 52–69). Two major lobbying groups have
developed, both dedicated to what they see as the need to preserve English against the perceived threat arising from increased
immigration. One group is the 100,000-member English First, of
Springfield, VA. The other, U.S. English, with 240,000 members,
was established in 1983 and traces its origins to then-senator S. I.
Hayakawa's 1981 proposed amendment to make English the official language of the United States. It grew out of the Federation
for American Immigration Reform, which received its funding
from a variety of sources, including the Pioneer Fund, a foundation dedicated in part to eugenics research. These two groups
provide the ideological and financial support for national and
local legislation to make English official and restrict use of other
languages.

Although English First and U.S. English are the main lobbying groups dedicated to this single issue, they are not the only
supportive organizations. Other groups supporting the national
English language amendment are the National Grange, the
American Legion, the National Confederation of American Eth-

nic Groups, the Polish American Congress, and the German American National Congress (National Education Association, 1988, pp. 11–12). In this combination of traditional patriotic and fraternal groups and organizations representing the "old" American immigration of the 19th century, we sense the appeal of official English legislation to those who, often despite their own immigrant origins, see the old order as changing and as changing in unpredictable, "anti-American" ways. Their rhetoric appeals to the same concerns that found expression in the language restrictions passed after World War I, as do allegations that language diversity creates social and political tensions. While such tensions may well coincide with language diversity, they are more likely to be a result rather than the cause of social and economic fragmentation. As Guy (1989) notes, "Language differences become politicized and divisive precisely when a dominant group tries to impose its language as an 'official' requirement" (p. 12).

Some individual members of language-minority groups have added their voices to the chorus supporting official designation or at least promotion of English because of their belief that bilingual education equals failure to learn English, which in turn prevents entry into the American mainstream. One is writer Richard Rodriguez (1982), whose autobiographical memoir calls acquisition of English a painful necessity and suggests that one must opt for either English or Spanish in 'the public sphere': To use both is not possible. Another, educator Rosalie Porter (1990), who entered school speaking mainly Italian, also sees the use of the native language as a crutch that retards academic development (see also discussion in the article by Pease-Alvarez and Hakuta in this issue). Both commentators take an either/or perspective on language. One must use one language *or* the other to deal with academic subjects.

Opposing English-only is the English Plus coalition, which promotes individual and group rights to use other languages. It was formed in 1988 through the efforts of the National Immigration, Refugee, and Citizenship Forum, an advocacy and civil rights group, and the Joint National Committee on Languages, itself a coalition of professional groups representing language teachers including the American Council on the Teaching of Foreign Languages, Teachers of English to Speakers of Other Languages (TESOL), and the National Council of Teachers of English (NCTE). English Plus promotes the freedom to use any language and the value of learning and using languages in addition to English. The constituent civil rights groups see language use as a basic freedom that ought not be constrained by law, following precedents of recognition of rights of members of minority groups. The positions of other organizations associated with English Plus illustrate another of the paradoxes associated with the bilingual debate: Educational organizations, even the two most closely associated with the teaching of English, the Committee on College Composition and Communication (an affiliate of NCTE) and TESOL, actively oppose English only (Daniels, 1990). Additional organizations representing linguists and modern-language teachers as well as bilingual educators (Hornberger, 1990, p. 13) and, recently, psychologists (American Psychological Association, 1990) have also allied themselves with English Plus. These educators, language teachers, and social service providers see native-language use as both an individual right and an essential means of accomplishing their superordinate goals, whether those be mastery of academic material or delivery of social and mental health services (Padilla et al., 1990). Since, according to all available data (Veltman, 1983), immigrants are indeed learning English, English Plus supporters hold that it is counterproductive to require the officialization of English, particularly if it restricts freedom to draw on the resources, individual and social, of the native language.

Institutionalization Despite Declining Federal Leadership

Even while federal support for bilingual education has declined and symbolic issues regarding presumed need for linguistic assimilation versus the value of bilingualism have come to the forefront, the world of professional educators has witnessed a growing recognition of the validity of bilingual instruction. Bilingual education has become rapidly institutionalized since the early 1970s, with not only ethnic advocacy but professional educational organizations now addressing matters of expertise in bilingual and second-language instruction. Twenty-nine of the 50 states now make explicit provision for licensure in bilingual education, while 36 offer certification in English-as-a-second-language instruction (McFarren, Valadez, Crandall, Palomo, & Gregoire, 1988; Teachers of English to Speakers of Other Languages, 1989). In general, states offering one of these certifications also offer the other, an institutional recognition that both kinds of services are useful in serving students whose native language is not English.

Major mainstream professional organizations such as the National Education Association and the American Federation of Teachers have articulated official positions that support bilingual education; others, such as the Association of Supervision and Curriculum Development, have not endorsed bilingual education explicitly but have published sympathetic materials to inform their membership of the issues (e.g., Association of Supervision and Curriculum Development, 1987). Organizations for administrators have also produced informational materials, either reprinting research articles (Phi Delta Kappa, 1988) or commissioning their own studies (e.g., Council of Chief State School Officers, 1990). Within AERA itself, the topic has assumed importance: For the first time, the *Handbook of research on teaching* includes a chapter on "Teaching bilingual learners" (Wong Fillmore & Valadez, 1986).

To summarize, the sources of social tension that shape the policy context for bilingual education are manifold: growing numbers of eligible students; shrinking federal financial support; a negative attitude toward immigrants; a more conservative social agenda affecting all federal programs; and growing awareness, and often acceptance, of the legitimacy of bilingual instruction on the part of professional educators. Sometimes strident, the contemporary debate surrounding bilingual education is simply the latest manifestation of the social tensions implicit in *e pluribus unum,* tensions that often overshadow the pertinent educational questions. As long as schools serve linguistically diverse students, as long as educators seek a variety of ways to teach these students, and as long as symbolic issues related to language persist in public consciousness, the debate will continue.

STUDENT LEADER A REFLECTION OF BILINGUAL MODEL[3]

Daniel Lemas has his hands full juggling calculus homework, college applications and work on his senior project.

Daniel wants to study nuclear or aerospace engineering and minor in music.

[3]Article by Lisa Davis, staffwriter from the *Phoenix Gazette,* 114: A1, A10 D 20 '93. Copyright © 1993 by the Phoenix Newspapers. Reprinted with permission.

As student body president of Calexico High School with a 3.7 grade-point average, he has a good chance of being accepted at several universities.

When he started school in America five years ago, Daniel couldn't speak a work of English. He was 11 years old and terrified.

"I didn't know what to expect," Daniel says. "I had no idea what it was like. Then I came to school and I realized that most of the people were like me."

Calexico, just north of the border from Mexicali, Mexico, is about 60 miles southwest of Yuma. Ninety percent of the students live in poverty. Nearly all are Hispanic. More than half came from Mexico. Like Daniel, they came to the United States with no English skills.

Nearly all of them will go to college.

Calexico schools have spent the last decade defying the odds. The district's 15 percent dropout rate is nearly a third of the national average for its demographics. More than 95 percent of Calexico's graduates go on to college.

Those who work and learn here attribute their success to high expectations and an acceptance of students' primary language.

Everyone in Calexico High School takes college-prep courses. Students who don't yet have a grasp of English take them in Spanish. More than half of Calexico's teachers are certified in bilingual education.

The English skills will come in time, administrators say. They are not willing to make the rest of their students' education wait.

"Yes, you do want them to speak English," says Emily Palacio, assistant superintendent for instruction in Calexico. "But you want them to have something to say."

Getting a Start

Students who speak little or no English can study math, science, history and social studies in Spanish. In the meantime, they take one of three levels of written and oral English as a second language (ESL) classes.

Five of Arizona's 220 school districts provide bilingual programs to about 6,368 students. None is as comprehensive as Calexico's, says Verma Pastor, director of bilingual education for Arizona.

Calexico students move into bilingual classes and eventually, into the English classrooms as their language skills progress. No one is placed in a remedial class because of a language problem.

When Daniel arrived in Calexico in the seventh grade, he spoke no English. He was placed in beginning-level ESL classes. His history, math and science classes were in Spanish.

Physical education, music and art are always taught entirely in English, so students can hear and participate in the language they're learning.

The next year, as Daniel's skills progressed, he moved to intermediate-level ESL classes, and a bilingual class for math. His other classes were taught in Spanish.

By the third year, Daniel began making the transition to English. All his classes were bilingual or in English. Daniel simultaneously moved into a third level of ESL classes—this time writing and reading.

"It's a little bit at a time. They go slow enough for you to catch on, but not so slow that you get bored," Daniel says.

"Then the classes are 50 percent in Spanish and English. You get used to it."

Calexico's bilingual curriculum was born a dozen years ago out of necessity and opportunity. The border town already was feeling an influx of migration from Mexico and was looking for some way to educate the growing number of children who entered its schools at various grade levels without English skills.

Experimental Work

The answer came in a five-year study sponsored by the California Department of Education. Through the study, Calexico and three other school districts let their schools be experiments of educators who believed that children could best learn a second language the way they learned the first.

Calexico began using a method known as "natural learning" to teach English to newcomers.

It allows for a "silent period," much like that of a young child before uttering his first words. During that time, students learn by listening to the people around them. Language, teachers say, will emerge naturally.

At this level, students attend beginning-level written and oral ESL classes. They may ask a question in Spanish, but the teacher always responds in English. They also learn by watching the language in action.

If a teacher tells them to stand up, the teacher stands up. If she tells them to sit down, she says it while sitting.

Visual Aids

Students in Gilbert Mendez's class stand near their desks and climb onto an imaginary bicycle. Mendez leads them in steps toward riding a bike amid some giggles and excited shouting of answers.

"OK, put your left hand on the left handlebar and your right hand on the seat," Mendez says, completing the midair charade.

"What are you going to do now? Put your right hand on the . . .?"

"Handlebar," the class answers.

"Which handlebar?"

"The right one."

Mendez's class has learned "left" and "right" in English, along with a few nouns for parts of the bicycle.

In another class, students are paired up and assigned to describe what their partners are wearing.

"She is wearing a 'played (plaid)' shirt," one student says.

"That's right, she is wearing a plaid (correct pronunciation) shirt," teacher Arnold Pachter replies. Students are corrected by using the proper pronunciation without pointing out their error.

The most difficult part of teaching a language, Pachter explains, is getting students past their inhibitions to speak.

In more advanced classes, students write essays and use improvisational theater to learn English.

"The whole point of this class is to make them feel like they can communicate," Pachter says. "Because once they get over the hump, they start communicating and correcting themselves."

Delicate Mix

Pachter's formula for success is twofold.

"They need to be pushed and they need to have their hand held at the same time," he says.

Teachers and administrators at Calexico are quick to admit that their method of language learning often takes longer than students who take all their classes in English. But the benefits, they say, are worth the wait.

"It will take them a little bit longer, but they are not losing content and not falling behind," Pachter says. "We want them to be completely fluent."

Education experts estimate that it takes six to eight years before a student is academically fluent in another language.

"We don't lose them," Calexico Principal Harry Pearson says. "Even migrant students find a way to stay here."

The school's rigorous curriculum and high standards leave little room for slacking off. But the emphasis here is not on test scores, it's on college entrance.

"Kids are coming here from backgrounds that prevent them from doing well on (standardized) tests," Calexico Superintendent Roberto Moreno says. "We're looking at other achievements, like how they're doing in class and how they're moving on."

Success Stories

They are moving on in droves.

Of the 370 students who graduated in 1993, 355 went to college. Most enrolled in a community college for financial reasons and proximity. About 49 went directly into universities, primarily in California.

Another five enrolled in technical or vocational schools and two entered the military.

About 74 percent of high school graduates in Arizona enrolled in college, according to Arizona Department of Education estimates.

"There's a lot of peer pressure on them to go to college, since the school has that kind of reputation," said Pearson, who taught at Calexico High School from 1969 to 1985, and then returned last year as principal.

Fueled by another state grant, the district is undergoing an overhaul of its curriculum and education delivery.

"We're not a status-quo district," Moreno says. "We're not satisfied with where we are. We have to keep up on research and evaluate where we want to be."

Moreno knows Calexico schools inside and out. He graduated from Calexico High School and returned as a teacher in 1968. Last year, he was named superintendent.

He remembers the fights that divided the community in 1969 when the school board took a "leap of faith" and began teaching its students in Spanish.

"Many people really don't like the idea of an American school teaching in Spanish," Moreno says. "Then there's the people who say that they went through school in English and they turned out just fine.

"What they ignore is where they might have been," Moreno says. "And the students who didn't make it."

Moreno argues that his students are going through a transition period and that the district is more fixed on education than on the language it comes in.

The district's commitment to providing an equal-access, college-preparatory curriculum has often been as costly as it was controversial.

Costly Gains

A few years ago, Calexico adopted a hands-on math curriculum developed at the University of California at Davis. It was only available in English. The district spent $9,000 to have the materials translated into Spanish.

"If we wait until someone does it for us, we are saying that our English-as-second-language students can wait while the others move forward," Palacio says. "It's a matter of do you want to provide equal access or don't you?"

Moreno says the district is simply committed to preparing its students for a university-level education, regardless of their English skills.

"It sends a message that this is important," Moreno says.

The district has spent more than two decades cultivating that message. It is unquestionably an integral part of this relatively small town, where you can see Mexico from most neighborhoods.

"There's a lot of support for students in this community," Moreno says. "We've sold them on the idea that school is important."

Most of Calexico's families have two parents, Moreno says. Most migrated from Mexicali and expect their children to do better and go further.

Hunting For Grants

Calexico has avoided many urban, inner-city problems, but gang influence is growing here.

And in a city with nearly 30 percent unemployment, Calexico's students are intimately aware of the ills of poverty. But lack of opportunity is no longer an issue.

Calexico pays for most of its programs through federal and state grants, which school officials hunt with a passion. The district's budget is not far from Arizona's $4,191-per-child spending average. Its elementary school classrooms average about 30 to 33 children. High school classes jump to about 34.

Teacher's aides have been nearly eliminated, primarily through attrition, while the district invests more money in curriculum and teachers, who earn an average $41,000 a year.

It seems to pay off.

"Now that I'm a senior, I tend to meditate more and look back on what I've gone through," Daniel says. "For me, it's been a really powerful experience. I'm very attached to school.

"I didn't want to be a senior," Daniel says. "I'm just now getting over having to graduate and leave."

SCIENCE STUDENTS WHO ARE STILL
LEARNING ENGLISH[4]

As undergraduates become increasingly diverse linguistically, faculty members across the disciplines will need to reconsider how they use the English language in their teaching. Many of the students now enrolling in college are immigrants or the children of immigrants; many are learning English at the same time they are taking mainstream academic courses taught in that unfamiliar language. The instruction of undergraduates of limited English proficiency presents a challenge whatever the discipline, but science courses present special challenges.

First, science has a reputation for being "hard" academically. As a result, students may study and work diligently and still earn low grades. The language of science is also concise and precise. It is not possible to bluff one's way through a science course, nor is the science classroom noted for its warm, supportive atmosphere. The concepts, the way of thinking, and the vocabulary challenge even the best-prepared students. Although many disciplines in the social sciences and the humanities have greatly increased their attention to student-centered pedagogy in recent years, science

[4]Article by Judith W. Rosenthal. From *The Chronicle of Higher Education* N 3, 1993. Copyright © 1993 by The Chronicle of Higher Education. Reprinted by permission.

instruction remains "authoritarian" and "hierarchical," with lecturing the primary mode of instruction.

According to data from the National Science Foundation, between 1977 and 1990 the number of bachelor's degrees earned in the physical sciences dropped 28.4 per cent and the number earned in the biological sciences dropped 29.8 per cent. To explain this trend, fingers have been pointed in many directions—at the poor quality of high-school math and science instruction, at the need for more hands-on research experience, or at the need for curricular revision. But somehow, the professor who week after week delivers the lectures has been absolved from any responsibility for whether or not students continue studying science or switch to other majors.

The special needs of undergraduates of limited English proficiency have been overlooked in recent calls for reform in undergraduate science education. Reform plans do acknowledge the changing demographics of U.S. society, stating the importance of making science, math, engineering, and technology education accessible to all students, regardless of "race, language, sex, or economic circumstances," as one report puts it. But how those demographics should affect faculty members' teaching is rarely discussed.

At colleges and universities, the total number of Asian, Hispanic, American Indian, and foreign undergraduates increased by more than 50 per cent (from 978,000 to 1,508,000) between 1980 and 1990. Most of this growth occurred in the Asian and Hispanic student populations, which grew by 91.7 per cent and 60.3 per cent respectively. The number of American Indian undergraduates increased by 20.3 per cent and foreign undergraduates by 8.7 per cent. Although no organization is keeping track of the actual number of undergraduates with limited proficiency in English, a recent report from the Center for the Study of Community Colleges showed that the fastest-growing subject taught at two-year colleges is English as a second language, commonly known as ESL.

The number of undergraduates whose native language is not English will increase even more as the millions of students enrolled in elementary and secondary schools who are non-native speakers move through the educational pipeline. During the last 10 years alone, according to the U.S. census, the number of Hispanics living in the United States increased by 53 per cent and the number of Asians by 108 per cent. Nearly 14 per cent of persons aged 5 and older "sometimes or always" speak a language other than English at home, and the percentages are higher in 12 states. The number of children aged 5 to 17 who do not speak English at home has increased by 38.4 per cent in the last decade.

Right now, the education of students whose native language is not English is being addressed at the two ends of the educational pipeline. Some elementary- and secondary-school students are receiving ESL and/or bilingual education as mandated by the Bilingual Education Act of 1968. Foreign-born teaching assistants also are receiving increased instruction in English because of complaints from undergraduates about their language abilities. But what about appropriate science instruction for the limited–English-proficient undergraduates who occupy the mid-section of the science pipeline?

Science instructors know little about how to teach students who are still learning English. They tend to have many misconceptions about how college students learn English as a second language.

The first is that ESL classes can completely prepare students for their mainstream coursework. Research has shown, however, that mastery of academic English requires about six years, and that even after students have completed their ESL studies, they know that they need additional help. For example, they have difficulty with speaking, reading, and understanding their textbooks, taking notes while listening to lectures, and writing papers.

A second myth is that undergraduate ESL students can "pick up" English by "osmosis." College students are not young children, who can absorb a new language more easily by being immersed in it. For college students, second-language acquisition is a lengthy, complex process that is dependent on many factors, including the learner's literacy in his or her native language, the learning environment, and exposure to comprehensible input in the new language. The kinds of language skills required for success in the college classroom go far beyond the ability to hold a casual conversation. To learn new subject matter in a second language and to compete in the mainstream classroom, ESL students must be able to read textbooks, understand lectures, take notes, write papers, take exams, and use a wide range of complex language skills that their native English-speaking classmates use automatically.

A third misunderstanding has to do with making errors.

When ESL students make mistakes as they write or speak English, it is often interpreted to mean that they are not trying hard enough to master English. However, the research on second-language acquisition clearly shows that the only way to master a new language is to use it, and that making errors is unavoidable. Interestingly, several studies have found that science professors, when compared to their colleagues in the social sciences, education, and humanities, are the least tolerant of the kinds of writing errors made by non–native-English speakers.

A fourth and related myth is that correcting the language errors of ESL students will help them to learn English. Contrary to what many faculty members believe, ESL students usually do not learn from error correction. In fact, done excessively, it may inhibit students from writing and speaking in English. Modeling correct English usage is more effective than correcting errors. For example, if an ESL student says, "I no able to learn nothing today," the teacher should skip the lecture on double negatives and instead reply, "You are not able to learn anything today?"

Similarly, getting out the red pen and correcting all written errors (spelling, grammar, word choices, etc.) is also ineffective. No one, not even native English speakers, can remember all the "rules" of our language. Most of the errors made by ESL students are "developmental"—that is, they are the same kinds of errors made by children who are learning English as their native language. Other errors are a result of interference by the student's native language.

Undergraduate science instruction can be improved in a variety of ways for students who are not yet proficient in English. Although little of what follows has been described in research literature, some colleges are beginning to adopt non-traditional approaches to facilitate science instruction for such undergraduates.

One approach is to train science faculty members to modify the traditional lecture-lab format so that students with limited English will more easily understand what is being taught. This means providing "comprehensible input." According to Stephen D. Krashen, professor of linguistics at the University of Southern California, "comprehensible input" means that the listener should be able to understand most (but not necessarily all) of the information being received. In the case of science instruction, comprehensible input would refer not only to the presentation of the scientific information but also to the way in which the English language is used to deliver this material. Instructors, for example, would try to speak clearly and at a reasonable rate, would write key terms on the chalkboard, and would give several examples or analogies to explain abstract concepts.

Another approach is to pair a science course with an ESL course and have the two instructors work closely together. The students in the science course may all be non-native speakers of English or a mixture of ESL and native English speakers. In either case, the science professor focuses on providing comprehensible input by selecting written materials appropriate to the students' reading levels in English, and on presenting well-organized lectures, using simplified sentence structure and avoiding slang and idioms. The ESL course emphasizes helping the non-native English speakers to use writing, reading, and speaking techniques, as well as cooperative learning groups, to master the scientific subject matter. For example, the students might retell what they learned in the previous lecture, in addition to asking and answering questions about the new material. They might use crossword puzzles and label diagrams to help them learn the scientific vocabulary and practice outlining the chapter in the textbook that presents the new material.

A third possibility is "sheltered" science classrooms. Enrollment in such classes is limited to intermediate-level ESL students. They are taught by instructors who have had training in teaching ESL students. The students also receive some type of academic support, such as tutorial sessions, help in developing study skills, assistance with vocabulary and reading assignments, or supplemental reading materials in their native language.

Another model is teaching introductory science to students in their native language while they are simultaneously enrolled in an ESL class. Although many educators are taken aback by bilingual higher education, it has proved to be an effective way to keep language-minority students in college. They can begin working toward their degrees, taking academic courses at the same time they are learning English.

In view of the linguistic diversity of today's undergraduates, it is unfortunate that such alternative ways of teaching students with limited English proficiency are not mentioned in recommendations to reform science education. Most science educators are not even aware of their existence. If scientists and other educators are sincerely interested in recruiting more underrepresented minority students, keeping them in college, and encouraging them to study the sciences, they must stop ignoring the role that language plays in science instruction and consider adopting some nontraditional ways of teaching the rapidly growing population of non-native English speakers.

"THE BABEL MYTH": THE ENGLISH-ONLY MOVEMENT AND ITS IMPLICATIONS FOR LIBRARIES[5]

The protection of the Constitution extends to all,—to those who speak other languages as well as those born with English on the tongue. Perhaps it would be highly advantageous if all had ready understanding of our ordinary speech, but this cannot be coerced by methods which conflict with the Constitution,—a desirable end cannot be promoted by prohibited means.

—*Meyer v. Nebraska*, 262 U.S. 390 (1923)

The movement to pass a constitutional amendment declaring English the official language of the United States initially seems an innocuous, commonsense effort to promote national unity by supporting America's English-language heritage. It is not a burning issue with the general public or one that people generally know much about. If you were to conduct a random survey on the street asking passersby if English should be declared the official language of the United States, the majority of the responses would very likely be along the lines of "Oh, you mean it isn't . . . ? Well, if it is not, it certainly should be." The fact that the United States does not have a national language policy comes as a surprise to the average American—and the rest of the world. Yet in the past decade the English-only/official-English question has become increasingly controversial in the legislatures, the courts, and the schools of this country. Touching on such issues as patriotism, immigration policy, and bilingual education, it continues to provoke bitter arguments and to spark fear and passion on both sides.

[5]Article by Ingrid Betancourt, head of multicultural services and collections at the Newark (New Jersey) Public Library. From *Wilson Library Bulletin* F '92. Copyright © 1992 by The H. W. Wilson Company. Reprinted by permission of the author.

Official English—Pro and Con

The issues surrounding the question of an official language for the United States are complex. They go beyond rational, practical, and political concerns into the emotional and ideological realms of what it means to be an American. Proponents of the law to declare English the official language of the United States contend that English is in danger of being displaced by other languages. They advocate stricter standards for assessing proficiency in English for naturalization, an end to bilingual ballots, and limitation on all but transitional bilingual education. They argue that speaking a language other than English reflects a divided national loyalty and that the lack of English-language proficiency prevents immigrants from entering the economic mainstream. And above all, advocates of official English charge that a polyglot society is a divided society. They point to Canada as an example of a bilingual society where the language issue remains unsettled, generating conflict and needless duplication of government services.

Opponents perceive the movement largely as a manifestation of xenophobia and suggest that it has emerged in part as a reaction to the ethnic revival of the 1970s and to the increasing immigrant presence in America. They argue that immigrants already have ample incentive to learn English and are doing so. English-language acquisition generally follows the traditional three-generation pattern across all nationalities: the immigrant generation tends to be mainly monolingual in the native tongue; the next generation is bilingual, with knowledge of both English and the parents' language; and for the third generation, the preferred language is English. A 1985 Rand Corporation study found that among first-generation Americans whose native tongue is Spanish, 90 percent are proficient in English and 50 percent of their children can't speak Spanish.

Groups opposing English-only assert that the public policy implications of such legislation would seriously affect the provision of vital services to limited-English-proficient members of society and in some cases violate First Amendment speech guarantees. Excluding other languages from public documents and government programs would jeopardize the fundamental rights of Americans who do not speak English to have equal access to essential government services and educational opportunities.

Observers of this debate see evidence of a deep nativist feeling fueling the official language movement in America. They point out that settled Americans have traditionally been reluctant to accept newcomers, regarding them as socially, racially, and economically inferior. Newer and more visible immigrants are perceived as less willing to assimilate than earlier generations, and more insistent on special concessions and on government handouts. These negative perceptions and attitudes find an easy focus on minority languages—obvious badges of ethnicity—and result in demands for the establishment of an official language in America.

The impulse to impose English and limit other languages has repeatedly arisen during periods of political or economic ferment, when non-English speakers have been targeted as subversive, unemployable or otherwise resistant to assimilation.

The English-Language Amendment

The question of an official language is being presented to the American people at the national level in the form of an English-Language Amendment (ELA) to the United States Constitution. The amendment was first proposed in 1981 by former California Senator S. I. Hayakawa and has been reintroduced repeatedly in Congress since then. Currently there are two English-only initiatives before the 102d Congress. HJ Res 81, an Amendment to the Constitution Proposing English as the Official Language of the United States, would amend the Constitution so that the United States and state governments would be prohibited from requiring the use of any language other than English. The second one, HR 123/S 434, the Language of Government Act, would amend Title 4 of the U.S. Code to declare English the official language of the government of the United States and specifies that the government must "have an affirmative obligation to protect, preserve and enhance the role of English as the official language of the U.S."

Various national organizations have been established to either promote or lobby against the adoption of the ELA and the passage of English-only legislation at the state level. Two of the more visible and active pro-English-only ones are U.S. English, located in Washington, D.C., and English First, based in Falls Church, Virginia. Groups that support the English language along with second-language study or minority-language maintenance have found a voice through The English Plus Information Clearinghouse (EPIC). EPIC is a coalition of fifty-six organizations established under the auspices of the National Immigration, Refugee and Citizenship Forum and the Joint National Committee for Languages to centralize and disseminate information on language rights and language policy.

English-only efforts have been more successful at the state level. Since 1981 sixteen states have passed legislation that either declares English the official language or limits the use of other languages. Illinois declared "American" its official language in 1923 and amended the statute in 1969, changing the term to "English." There have been efforts to enact similar legislation at the state level in almost two dozen additional states.

On the other hand, four states—Oregon, Washington, New Mexico, and Hawaii—have passed English-plus amendments, resolutions, or statutes endorsing cultural diversity and the use of various languages in business, government, and private affairs as official state policies. In 1990 a federal court ruled that Arizona's recently adopted English-only statute, which read, "This state and all political subdivisions of this state shall act in English and no other language," violated First Amendment speech rights. The statute was revoked.

Hostility and Intolerance

The affirmation that the English-only campaign is a moderate movement seeking to promote national unity appeared plausible until the passage of English-only laws at the state and local levels. In the aftermath of California's Proposition 63—a constitutional amendment passed in 1986 making English the official language of the state—and similar measures in Colorado, Florida, and elsewhere, it has become clear that English-only policies encourage hostility toward immigrants and increase intolerance toward citizens, especially Asians and Latinos, whose first language is not English.

The establishment of English as the official language in these states has given legitimacy to the English-only regulations that an increasing number of organizations and businesses have begun to implement. Many anti-immigrant and anti-minority-language incidents have been reported in the press. In California, Huntington Park municipal court employees were forbidden to talk to each other in Spanish while on the job. After the employees challenged this policy, the Ninth U.S. Circuit Court ruled the ban illegal. The court found the regulation to be discriminatory, fos-

tering "an atmosphere of inferiority, isolation and intimidation."
At a hospital in Los Angeles, workers were prohibited from
speaking any language but English and urged to report anyone
who violated the ban. The manager of an insurance company
ordered employees not to converse in Chinese unless dealing with
a Chinese-speaking customer.

Passage of the Colorado official-English amendment to the
state's constitution prompted a wave of anti-Hispanic discrimination. The *Chicago Tribune* reported that a school bus driver forbade children to speak Spanish on the bus and that a restaurant
worker was fired for translating menu items into Spanish for
customers from Latin America. The Associated Press ran a story
recounting the suspension of a supermarket cashier in Miami for
speaking Spanish on the job to a fellow employee. Although the
supermarket chain denies that the suspension was based on linguistic grounds, the cashier insists that the written notice clearly
stated that the suspension was for "speaking a foreign language."

In response to the proliferation of English-only rules in the
workplace, a bill prohibiting such policies was recently introduced
in the California legislature. If passed, the bill (SB 834) would
prohibit employers from adopting English-only rules unless they
are justified by business necessity.

Although English is the common, national language of the
United States, it is not, nor has it ever been, the exclusive language spoken in the country. In addition to the various native
American languages in use on the continent prior to European
settlement and the Dutch, French, Hawaiian, Spanish, and Tagalog that coexisted with English in the territories, there are the
myriad languages of the people who came to build America—
willingly or under duress. In the case of French in the Louisiana
territory and Spanish in the West, Southwest, and Puerto Rico,
the languages did not knock at America's doors, but rather the
country reached out to encompass, if not embrace them.

The case of Puerto Rico is particularly interesting. The
island-country became a United States territory in 1898 as a result
of the Spanish-American War. The Jones Act of 1917 granted de
facto United States citizenship to all Puerto Ricans, whether resid-
ing on the island or the U.S. mainland, without an English-
language requirement. At that point in history, Puerto Ricans
possessed four centuries of Spanish language and native American, African, and European heritage. In its formal Language
Policy the National Puerto Rican Coalition (NPRC) articulates the

premise that Puerto Ricans' right to full American citizenship in the context of their own language and culture has been guaranteed by law.

Puerto Rico's compact of association with the United States, and subsequent legislation and judicial opinions, recognizes the status of Puerto Ricans as Spanish-speaking Americans. Together with other native-born Americans whose first language is not English, they have a right to exercise the prerogatives of citizenship in their language if they need to.

Impact on Libraries

English-only laws have begun to have a chilling effect on the provision of library and information services to speakers of other languages. Public libraries are finding it necessary to review their policies and articulate, clearly and solidly, their charge to serve all members of the community, regardless of linguistic background.

Monterey Park, California is an interesting case in point. A town of 60,000 residents located just a few minutes to the east of downtown Los Angeles, Monterey Park has a population that is three-quarters Asian. The *Los Angeles Times* called it "the first suburban Chinatown." In 1987 a slate of candidates who had pledged to put teeth into Proposition 63 (which had been approved the year before) was elected to the Monterey Park City Council. When the library was offered a gift of ten thousand Chinese books, the mayor, with the support of the city council, tried to block the library from accepting the donation. At the time the Chinese collection made up less than 10 percent of the library's total holdings. The library board stood by its decision to accept the gift and defended the library's collection development policy. In response, the city council dissolved the library's independent board of commissioners and took control of library management. Although the council used "financial accountability" as a justification, it was clear that its actions had a more disturbing motivation. The mayor of Monterey Park was surprisingly frank about his view that the public library's services should be extended only to citizens able to read English. "I don't think we need to cater too much to foreign languages. I think if people want a foreign language they can go purchase books on their own," the mayor was quoted as saying in the *Los Angeles Times*.

Concerned citizens and civil liberties groups filed a lawsuit in the Superior Court. After considerable litigation and much public controversy they won the case and the library board was reinstated.

But sobering as the English-only movement has been, it has also served to rally the library profession around one of its most fundamental tenets: meeting the educational, cultural, and recreational needs of *all members* of the community. In response to the escalating English-only crusade, the American Library Association passed a resolution in 1983 supporting the provision of equitable levels of library service to all members of the community regardless of ethnic, cultural, or linguistic background. Similar resolutions have been passed by the library associations of California, New Jersey, and several other states.

Pivotal ventures are taking place at the state level as well. In 1987 the California State Library funded a committee to design and organize the statewide conference, State of Change: California's Ethnic Future and Libraries, which examined the need for new policies and approaches to address the state's growing diversity. The state library is now using the information, ideas, and energy generated by the conference to spearhead the Partnerships for Change Program to assist public libraries in their efforts to improve services to ethnic and racial constituents.

In addition, other state libraries have begun to take dynamic steps to insure that local libraries are equipped to meet the challenges inherent in serving multicultural and multilingual communities. By guiding local libraries through the twin processes of community assessment and short- and long-term planning, and by providing the necessary information, training, and financial resources, some state libraries are giving invaluable support to local libraries in their efforts to adapt to a rapidly changing clientele.

Outlook for the Future

The question of an official language for America has generated controversy and impassioned debate since the founding of the country two centuries ago. The fact that the framers of the Constitution neglected to proclaim an official language is regarded by some as a deliberate omission, a refusal to institute a dictate that would be both culturally and politically divisive.

The United States of America has always been a multilingual nation with English as the cardinal, common language. Over 97 percent of the population of the United States speak English. We need to examine whether English, the language of government, of the laws, of the courts, of commerce—the language of power—

is in any danger of being obliterated in this country or whether it is minority languages that are fated to wane in a couple of generations because of the constant onslaught of English from every conceivable angle.

But, above all, we need to examine the authentic benefits—other than its implicit symbolic value—of an English-Language Amendment. Is it going to expedite the adoption of English by non- or limited-English speakers? Unlikely, since colleges, adult education programs, and public libraries are currently unable to meet the overwhelming demand for adequate English-as-a-second-language instruction and materials. A constitutional amendment is not going to force people to speak English if they are unable or unwilling to do so. Is the ELA going to eliminate the use of minority languages in the United States? Obviously not. It is impossible to legislate assimilation. By definition, it is a process that happens gradually over time.

Repressive measures taken against minority languages have done extraordinarily little to promote national unity. Historically, such decrees have had quite the opposite results, creating divisiveness and defiance. Witness the historically unsuccessful attempts of the Spanish government to suppress Catalan and Basque, as well as the opposition to Russian and the current resurgence of ethnic languages in the Soviet Union.

The United States is losing its competitive edge in an increasingly interdependent and interconnected world because of linguistic myopia. In his book *The Tongue-Tied American,* Senator Paul Simon of Illinois discusses the negative impact that the reluctance of Americans to study other languages is having on the United States' ability to deal efficiently with other countries, politically and economically. The economic revival of the formerly run-down Miami Beach area is attributed to the large influx of capital generated by Spanish-English bilingual entrepreneurs in the region who were able to attract business and investment from Latin America. The state of Utah, likewise, has been successful in attracting foreign investment because so many of its people become fluent in foreign languages while serving as Mormon missionaries.

The United States needs a national language policy. But rather than establishing a policy of exclusion, such a document needs to encompass, respect, and protect the rights of minority-language speakers and needs to engender societal and educational support for the maintenance and learning of other languages in America.

It is a good guess that with or without the passage of English-language laws, English will continue to grow and thrive in the United States. The real question is, how will the United States respond to the social and political forces propelling this country towards the twenty-first century in an increasingly interdependent and interconnected world?

A STORY OF TWO CHILDREN[6]

When President Clinton and Vice-President Gore talk about the need to reinvent government, there is a tendency to dismiss this as a catch phrase. That's a mistake; it's an effort to deal with a serious problem that can and should be dealt with. Most people agree there are problems that federal, state or local government should be handling. However, they have doubts that government can handle them sensibly and effectively. Their doubts are well-founded.

Over 20 years ago, a judge decided it was not fair that a young Chinese boy named Kinney Lau who didn't understand English had to get his education in classes where only English was spoken. The Supreme Court agreed in a decision called *Lau v. Nichols*. It said that providing Kinney Lau with instruction only in English was the same thing as denying him an education.

This decision stimulated the establishment of a variety of programs, including bilingual education, all over the country. The idea of bilingual education—teaching kids in a language they could understand while they were making the transition between their native language and English—was a good one. The sink-or-swim approach to learning English that we once employed with immigrant children was very rough. Almost all children are frightened when they first leave the familiar atmosphere of home to go to school, but for the child who does not speak English, the experience can be terrifying and lead to a permanent dislike of school and learning. Bilingual programs can help by allowing these kids to learn some of their subjects in their native language

[6]Column by Albert Shanker, President of the American Federation of Teachers. From the *New York Times*, E7 D 26 '93. Copyright © 1993, Albert Shanker. Reprinted with permission.

while they are learning English. Also, while insisting that they do learn English, bilingual programs can get across the idea that these youngsters should be proud of their origins rather than ashamed of being different, as many youngsters used to be.

But the rules and regulations used to administer bilingual education programs can create the same kind of obstacles to educational opportunity that the law intended to remove. For example, the *New York Times* recently told the story of how a Hispanic-surnamed child who spoke only English was assigned to a class that was taught almost entirely in Spanish ("School Programs Assailed as Bilingual Bureaucracy" by Joseph Berger, January 4, 1993). Vanessa Correa was put in exactly the same spot as Kinney Lau, the young Chinese boy—she was stuck in a class where she could not understand what was going on.

Was Vanessa the victim of some sort of snafu? As a matter of fact, assigning the English-speaking child to a class where she would be taught in Spanish was entirely in accordance with the rules of the bilingual program. The child had a Hispanic surname and a test showed her to be below average in English, and that was enough. That she was born in this country and spoke no Spanish didn't matter. And it wouldn't have mattered if she had been equally poor in English and Spanish or if her Spanish had been much poorer than her English. The rule would still have placed her in a Spanish-language class.

When Vanessa's parents, fluent speakers of English, complained about the placement, the bureaucratic machine groaned into action and put the child into a class for students who had English as a second language. Given the rules, there was no way of getting her into a regular class where she could learn her native language—English—along with other youngsters who were native speakers. The way the bilingual education law was administered recreated the problem the law was intended to solve. So much for the spirit of the *Lau* decision.

This story happened to take place in New York City, but it is not a New York story. The same thing happens in bilingual education everywhere. And the same thing happens with many other well-intentioned government programs.

In recent years, conservatives have taken advantage of stories like Vanessa's to attack the value of all government social programs. They say that any time the government—federal, state or local—undertakes a program, it turns the program into a mess. The public generally recognizes that things like day care or health

care are essential and are unlikely to get done unless the government undertakes them. But when they look at some of the disas-
ters, they have second thoughts.

The solution is not to do away with the government's role in
solving social problems but to do away with the stupid rules that
govern many programs. Not only do these rules create incentives
to lose sight of the individuals they are supposed to help; they also
undermine good programs and can ultimately destroy them. It
has been a year since Vanessa Correa's story made the front page
of the *New York Times*. Has the rule that landed her in a class
where she could not understand what was going on been
changed? I doubt it.

BIBLIOGRAPHY

An asterisk (*) preceding a reference indicates an excerpt from the work has been reprinted in this book.

BOOKS AND PAMPHLETS

Adams, K. L. & Brink, D. T., eds. Perspectives on official English: the campaign for English as the official language of the USA. Mouton de Gruyter. '90.

Alatis, J. E., ed. Georgetown University round table on languages and linguistics. Georgetown University Press. '78.

August, Diane & Garcia, Eugene E. Language minority education in the United States. Charles C. Thomas. '88.

Baker, K. & deKanter, A., eds. Bilingual education: a reappraisal of federal policy. D. C. Heath. '83.

Baron, Dennis E. The English-only question: an official language for Americans? Yale University Press. '90.

Beer, W. R. & Jacob, J. E. Language policy and national unity. Rowman & Allanheld. '85.

Bikales, Gerda & Imhoff, Gary. A Kind of discordant harmony: issues in assimilation. U.S. English. '85.

Butler, R. E. On creating a Hispanic America: a nation within a nation? Council for Inter-American Security. '85.

Cafferty, Pastora San Juan & Rivera-Martinez, Carmen. The politics of language: the dilemma of bilingual education for Puerto Ricans. Westview. '81.

Cheshire, J., ed. English around the world: sociolinguistic perspectives. Cambridge University Press. '91.

Cline, H. H. Is there a hidden agenda? The English language amendment. City College of the City University of New York. '89.

Cobarrubias, J. & Fishman, Joshua A., eds. Progress in language planning: international perspectives. Mouton. '83.

Conklin, N. F. & Lourie, M. A. A host of tongues: language communities in the United States. Free Press. '83.

Connor, E., ed. Mexican-Americans in comparative perspective. Urban Institute. '85.

Cooper, R. L. Language planning and social change. Cambridge University Press. '89.

Crawford, James. Bilingual education: history, politics, theory, and practice. Crane. '89.

Crawford, James. Hold your tongue: bilingualism and the politics of "English only". Addison-Wesley. '92.

Crawford, James. Language loyalties: a sourcebook on the official English controversy. University of Chicago Press. '92.

Daniels, Harvey A., ed. Not only English: affirming America's multilingual heritage. National Council of Teachers of English. '90.

Dharmadhikari, S. The official English movement in New York and in the nation. New York City Department of City Planning. '89.

English language amendment: hearings on Senate Joint Resolution 167 before the subcommittee on the Constitution of the Senate Judiciary Committee. U.S. Senate, 98th Congress, 2nd session, 1984. U.S. Government Printing Office. '84.

English only movement: an agenda for discrimination. League of United Latin American Citizens. '86.

English plus: legislative packet for municipal/county officials. NALEO Education Fund. '89.

Estudios Chicanos and the politics of community: Selected proceedings. National Association for Chicano Studies. '89.

Ferguson, Charles A. & Heath, Shirley Brice. Language in the USA. Cambridge University Press. '80.

Fishman, Joshua A. et al. Language loyalty in the United States: the maintenance and perpetuation of non-English mother tongues by American ethnic and religious groups. Arno. '78.

Ford, M. L. One language for the United States? Un idioma para los Estados Unidos? Council of State Governments. '84.

Graham, H. D. American liberalism and language policy: should liberals support official English? U.S. English, '90.

Grosjean, F. Life with two languages: an introduction to bilingualism. Harvard University Press. '82.

Hakuta, K. Mirror of language: the debate on bilingualism. Basic. '86.

Harlan, J. Bilingualism in the United States. Franklin Watts. '91.

*Hayakawa, S. I. The English Language Amendment: one nation . . . indivisible? Washington Institute for Values in Public Policy, Inc. '85.

Hero, R. E. Latinos and the U.S. political system: two-tiered pluralism. Temple University Press. '92.

Hirsch, E. D., Jr. Cultural literacy: what every American needs to know. Houghton Mifflin. '87.

Imhoff, Gary, ed. Learning in two languages: from conflict to consensus in the reorganization of schools. Transaction. '90.

Imhoff, Gary & Lamm, R. D. Immigration time bomb: the fragmenting of America. Truman Talley. '85.

Kachru, B. B. Other tongue: English across cultures. University of Illinois Press. '81.

Kloss, H. The American bilingual tradition. Newbury House. '77.

Knepler, H. & Knepler, M. Crossing cultures. Macmillan. '87.

Kritz, M. M. ed. U.S. immigration policy and refugee policy. Lexington. '83.

Language and the state: the law and politics of identity: proceedings of the second National Conference on Constitutional Affairs. Les Editions Yvon Blais Inc. '91.

Levine, M. V. Reconquest of Montreal: language policy and social change in a bilingual city. Temple University Press. '90.

Macias, Reynaldo F., ed. Are English language amendments in the national interest? A policy analysis of proposals to establish English as the official language of the United States. Tomas Rivera Center. '88.

McKay, S. L. & Wong, S. C. Language diversity: problem or resource: A Social & educational perspective on language minorities in the United States. Harper & Row. '88.

O'Barr, W. M. & O'Barr, J. F., eds. Language and politics. Mouton. '76.

Padilla, Amado M., et al., eds. Bilingual education: issues and strategies. Sage. '90.

Paral, R. English only: the threat of language restrictions. National Association of Latino Elected and Appointed Officials. '89.

Phillips, J. K. The language connection: from the classroom to the world. National Textbook. '77.

Piatt, B. Only English?: law and language policy in the United States. University of New Mexico Press. '90.

Porter, R. P. Forked tongue: the politics of education. Basic. '90.

Ridge, Martin, ed. The new bilingualism: an American dilemma. Transaction. '81.

San Miguel, G. One country, one languages: A historical sketch of English language movements in the United States. Tomas Rivera Center. '86.

Simpson, D. Politics of American English, 1776–1850. Oxford University Press. '86.

Stein, Colman Brez Jr. Sink or swim: the politics of bilingual education. Praeger. '86.

Trasvina, John. Official English/English only: more than meets the eye. National Education Association. '88.

Troike, R. Research evidence for the effectiveness of bilingual education. National Dissemination and Assessment Center. '78.

Veltman, Calvin. The future of the Spanish language in the United States. Hispanic Policy Development Center. '88.

Wardhaugh, R. Language and nationhood: the Canadian experience. New Star. '83.

For those who wish to read more widely on the subject of language and language policy, this section contains abstracts of additional articles that bear on the topic. Readers who require a comprehensive list of materials are advised to consult the *Reader's Guide to Periodical Literature* and other Wilson indexes.

Echoes of nativism (official English referendums). *America* 159:483 D 10 '88

The passage of statutes or constitutional amendments in Arizona, Colorado, and Florida declaring English the states' official language and limiting the use of any other language in governmental business was motivated by ethnocentricity and xenophobia. Advocates of "official English" appear disingenuous when they urge the elimination of bilingual education programs from the public schools, since the best evidence suggests that children of Hispanic and Asian families want to learn English and do so. The recent resignation of John Tanton as chairman of U.S. English, the chief lobbyist for this year's "English only" proposals, indicates that ethnic bias is at work in the movement. The resignation followed the public revelation of a memorandum in which Tanton claimed that the high birth rate among Hispanics threatened non-Hispanic whites.

Official English: fear or foresight? Nancy Bane, *America* 159:515–16+ D 17 '88

The ability to communicate in English is the only sure means of winning jobs, money, and a better life in the United States. Bilingual education was once seen as an ideal way to help immigrants learn English with as little cultural shock as possible. This method only lengthens the time it takes immigrants to enter mainstream America, however, and it sometimes fosters increased dependence on native languages. Colorado recently passed a law establishing English as the official language of the state. The law is not intended to homogenize various ethnic cultures but rather to ensure that the state's citizens have a common means of communication.

U.S. language debate rages. Eleanor Branch, *Black Enterprise* 17:20+ Jl '87

A movement begun by former California senator S. I. Hayakawa to make English the official language of the United States has gathered momentum. Official language legislation was passed in California last November, and legislation supporting the official language movement has been reintroduced in Congress. Opponents of the legislation argue that it jeopardizes the notion of a pluralistic society by excluding multilingualism from

American politics, media, and free enterprise. Proponents claim that it merely reaffirms the need for a common language.

Should English-only be the law of the land? Elizabeth Ehrlich, *Business Week* 116+ N 10 '86

U.S. English (USE), a national organization formed by former senator S. I. Hayakawa of California, is campaigning to make English the official language of the United States. The movement's first test will come on November 4, when California will vote on whether to make English the state's official tongue. Gerda Bikales, executive director of USE, argues that an official language reinforces the connection between individuals and strengthens the national identity, and he points to the self-sufficient barrios of Miami and Los Angeles as examples of places where Hispanics have no cultural connection with the larger society. Opponents of the measure, which include the American Civil Liberties Union, argue that the amendment is vague and could lead to many lawsuits. They also fear that the amendment will disenfranchise voters by doing away with bilingual ballots.

Outlawing tongues. David R. Carlin, Jr., *Commonweal* 113:648–9 D 5 '86

The English Language Amendment, passed by voters in California to make English the state's official language, is a superfluous measure. Although the amendment's proponents, led by former Republican senator S. I. Hayakawa, correctly see the social advantages of linguistic homogeneity, they have no serious evidence that English is losing ground in America. Attempts to compel linguistic assimilation will only increase the attachment of non-English speaking people to their stigmatized languages. Linguistic preference is determined by love of a language, not by laws.

Why English should be our official language. S. I. Hayakawa, *The Education Digest* 52:36–7 My '87

Condensed from an article in the January 1987 issue of the Executive Educator. In recent years, resistance to America's "melting pot" ideal has arisen, especially among those who claim to speak for the country's Hispanic-American citizens. They support a "salad bowl" ideal in which different elements mingle while retaining their distinctive characters. Key in their agenda is the use of bilingual education to encourage the use of Spanish among Hispanic-Americans. This is a dangerous idea that could split the United States into a bicultural society. English should be established as the country's official language. If it is to be truly useful, bilingual education must be chosen freely by local school authorities and must prepare students for transfer to a standard classroom after not more than two years. Millions of immigrants over the years have learned English and assimilated into the mainstream, and today's immigrants can do the same.

Bilingualism: a wolf in sheep's clothing. Howard Banks, *Forbes 145:64 Je 11 '90*

Former senator S. I. Hayakawa launched the campaign for a constitutional amendment to make English the official language of the United States in 1981. The 1974 Bilingual Education Act had for the first time encouraged people not to learn English. To Hayakawa's mind, this threatens the great American experiment, where a vibrant new culture is largely the result of the use of a common language. His amendment would clear away the mixed signals given to immigrants since the 1970s.

English: the language of liberty. J. R. Joelson, *The Humanist 49:35–6 Jl/Ag '89*

Opponents and proponents of legislation that would establish English as the official language of the United States ignore the crucial facts that language, culture, and politics cannot be separated and that English is the language of Americans' political freedom. Essential principles of liberty established by the Constitution, the Declaration of Independence, the Bill of Rights, the Emancipation Proclamation, the 14th Amendment, and the 1964 Civil Rights Act have all been framed in English. Establishing English as the official language would preserve America's political values for posterity.

English-only is backward step Calif. solon Brown says [views of W. Brown on making English the official language of California]. *Jet 70:6 S 1 '86*

California Assembly Speaker Willie Brown maintains that passage of a proposition that would make English the official language of California would be a serious setback to bilingual education.

A tougher language bill [bilingualism requirements in Canada]. Paul Gessell, *Maclean's 100:15 Jl 6 '87*

A new bill designed to promote greater linguistic equality among Canadians appears to enjoy widespread political support, but its full impact will not be known for months. The new official languages bill imposes bilingual requirements on federal agencies and some courts so that people can work for or be served by the government in either official language. The bill also calls for the expenditure of $25 million over three years to promote bilingualism in the delivery of provincial and municipal health and social services.

Accents of conflict: the melting pot menaces linguistic minorities. Barry Came, *Maclean's* 103:77+ Je 25 '90

Part of a special section examining attitudes in Canada and the United States. Minority languages in Canada and the United States are threatened. Outside Quebec, the number of people whose native language is French is declining, while English-speaking communities have all but disappeared everywhere in Quebec outside Montreal. In the United States, minority languages are perpetuated largely by immigrants, but those languages are under attack. In the Maclean's/Decima Portrait of Two Nations poll, the majority of Canadians and Americans said that Canada is a place where languages other than English are accepted. Unlike Canada, the United States has not taken legislative steps to preserve minority languages. Instead, bilingual education is opposed in the United States by groups seeking recognition of English as the official national language. So far, 18 U.S. states have declared themselves unilingually English.

Anger at the core [Confederation of Regions party wins opposition status in New Brunswick on English-only platform]. Paul Kaihla, *Maclean's* 104:16–18 O 7 '91

In a stunning upset, the Confederation of Regions (CoR) Party recently won opposition status in New Brunswick premier Frank McKenna's Liberal government. Election results found the Liberal Party holding an impressive 46 seats; the Conservatives, just 3; the New Democratic Party, 1; and the CoR, an unprecedented 8. CoR, which was established seven years ago and has been a fringe party until now, espouses the abolition of official bilingualism and the establishment of English as Canada's only official language; the combining of Canada's ten provinces into four jurisdictions—the West, Ontario, Quebec, and the Atlantic region; free votes on such issues as abortion and capital punishment; and the right of voters to recall local MPs or senators whose voting record strays from majority opinion. CoR's success will undoubtedly inflame long-standing bilingual tensions in the province, where about one-third of the residents speak French.

The new apartheid. *National Review* 42:14–16 Jl 23 '90

Advocates of bilingual education and the people whom such education is supposed to benefit are increasingly at odds. A recent San Francisco Chronicle survey of minority residents in the Bay Area suggests that the majority of respondents believe that English should be the official language of California. Nevertheless, bilingual education advocates are intensifying their efforts to keep English from taking root. Most recently, they have been lobbying Capitol Hill to prevent such early childhood education programs as Head Start from being conducted exclusively in English, which is best learned at an early age.

Are you talking to me? Lionel Chetwynd, *National Review* 45:72
Ag 9 '93

The Great American Experiment has proved a great refuge for millions
of Europeans and can continue to do so today for immigrants from elsewhere in the world. It is necessary, however, for the new immigrants to do
as past immigrants have done—respect the individual rights of others,
accept English as the common tongue, and believe in human dignity.

The American creed: from dilemma to decomposition. Arthur M.
Schlesinger, *New Perspectives Quarterly* 8:20–5 Summ '91

Part of a special issue on racism. The cult of ethnicity that began as a
protest against Anglocentric culture is threatening to become a counter-
revolution against the original theory of America as a single nation with a
common culture. The cult exaggerates differences, fuels antagonisms and
resentments, and separates races and nationalities, leading to self pity and
self ghettoization. Unexpectedly, blacks are demanding the return of
black-white segregation, beginning in the schools. The separatist impulse,
however, isn't confined to the black community. It is also finding expression in the bilingualist movement, which is being driven by Hispanic
Americans. In American society, those who use a language other than
English are doomed to second class citizenship. In a country as hetero-
geneous as America, national cohesion requires a common language.

Los Angeles schools to hire bilingual teachers from Mexico.
New York Times B9 Ag 4 '93

The Los Angeles school board and the Mexican government have agreed
to place 20 bilingual teachers from Mexico in Spanish-speaking jobs in the
Los Angeles School District this fall. Leticia Quezada, the board president, says that the district has found it difficult to fill the 2,500 job open-
ings that exist for Spanish-speaking teachers.

Say it in English. Eloise Salholz, *Newsweek* 113:22–3 F 20 '89

The U.S. Constitution does not provide for an official language, and
tongues other than English have always been spoken in America. In recent years, however, resentment of non-English speakers has grown, and
17 states have made English their official language. In some cases such
laws have little more than symbolic significance, but they have the potential to make a broad impact on daily life and the law. The force behind this
movement is U.S. English, an organization that fears that the country may
become linguistically and culturally divided. The group wants a constitutional amendment making English the official language and also advocates such measures as eliminating non-English voting ballots and restricting bilingual-education programs. Supporters of the group argue that

recent immigrants do not want to enter the American mainstream. Opponents dispute this contention and charge that the issue is a cover for bigotry.

A special section on educating immigrant children [with editorial comment by Pauline B. Gough]. *Phi Delta Kappan* 70:186, 199–225 N '88

A special section discusses the education of immigrant children. Immigration to the United States in the 1980s is expected to match or exceed the record of nearly 9 million set between 1900 and 1910. While most of the earlier immigrants were unskilled laborers from Europe, the new arrivals are primarily Hispanic or Asian and have diverse skills. The current immigrants may find integration into American society harder than their forebears did. For example, a growing "English only" movement, which wants to establish English as the official language for the conduct of public affairs, could result in the exclusion of immigrants from police, health, and fire services; from the courts; and from equal opportunities in education. Articles discuss immigrant children in California, the destructive stereotyping of Asian American students, the challenges posed by immigrant students, and ways that schools and educators can work effectively with Asian immigrant parents.

Bilingual education. Karen N. Peart, *Scholastic Update* (Teachers' edition) 126:22 N 19 '93

Part of an issue on immigration. Bilingual education is one area of public debate concerning immigration. Those who favor such programs say that non-English speakers perform better if they are taught in their native language and learn English at a relaxed pace; some studies show that developing skills in a native language leads to quicker development in English. Backers of bilingual programs also contend that they produce students fluent in 2 languages, a skill that gives them a competitive edge in today's diverse society. Critics of bilingual education maintain that these programs produce students who are not fluent in English, hindering their assimilation into the mainstream and putting them at a disadvantage.

English spoken here, O.K.? Jay Carney, *Time* 128:27 Ag 25 '86

The merits of bilingualism are being debated in California as a campaign to make English the state's official language gathers force. Proposition 63 will come before the voters in November. Opponents of the resolution charge that it fosters racism and xenophobia, while supporters claim that bilingualism is a barrier to national unity. Three California towns have already adopted English as their official language. A Washington-based group called U.S. English is gathering support for a constitutional amendment to make English the nation's official language.

Only English spoken here. Margaret B. Carlson, *Time* 132:29 D 5 '88

U.S. English, a group that has sponsored state initiatives declaring English the official language and that wants a constitutional amendment to that effect, represents a growing feeling that the mother tongue needs protection. In particular, the cohesiveness and political power of Hispanic immigrants has unnerved some Americans. U.S. English advocates stricter standards for assessing proficiency in English for naturalization, an end to bilingual ballots, and limitations on all but "transitional" bilingual education. Opponents see the movement as a simple manifestation of xenophobia. Their argument is supported by a 1986 memo written by U.S. English co-founder John Tanton, who has since been forced to leave, expressing concern that Hispanics would someday outnumber whites.

No official language. *Time* 135:82 F 19 '90

A federal court has struck down Arizona's official English law, which had required state and local governments to conduct their business in English. A state court had earlier upheld the provision, but federal district judge Paul Rosenblatt ruled that the law violated the First Amendment. The lawsuit was originally filed by Maria-Kelly Yniguez, a state insurance-claims manager who feared retribution if she spoke Spanish to coworkers or claimants. Advocates of language pluralism contend that English-only laws are thinly disguised and discriminatory anti-immigrant measures.

Bilingualism in America: English should be the only language. S. I. Hayakawa, *USA Today* (Periodical) 118:32–4 Jl '89

English should be made the official language of the United States. A common language is a unifying force that allows citizens to become informed members of the electorate. In countries like India and Belgium, multilingualism has contributed to chaos and political instability. Maintaining legally mandated bilingual services costs about $400 million a year in Canada and could run into the billions in the United States. Bilingual education is fine if it encourages newcomers to learn English, but it often does the opposite. One of the aspects of the bilingual movement, the effort to require bilingual ballots, is racist in its underlying assumption that people of certain races are not smart enough to learn English.

Don't put the accent on bigotry [movement to make English the official language of the United States]. Robert E. Burns, *U.S. Catholic* 55:2 Ag '90

The movement to have English declared the official language of the United States is aimed at stamping out bilingualism. Supporters of this movement claim that bilingual services are a waste of taxpayers' money, but this argument is hardly persuasive coming from people who ignore the billions of tax dollars used to pay for unnecessary weapons systems. The rationale for bilingualism in schools and other places is to bridge the gap facing new immigrants. In schools where bilingual programs are in place, non-English-speaking children are taught in their native languages at the same academic level as their English-speaking classmates so that they will not be behind when they are phased into regular classes.

A war over words. Susanna McBee, *U.S. News & World Report* 101:64 O 6 '86

The influx of non-English-speaking immigrants into the United States over recent years has spurred a growing movement to declare English the country's official language. Those who support the movement say that a common language is needed to maintain the nation's common bonds; some ethnic groups, however, feel that a move to enforce a common language could promote racism. Voters in California will vote on Proposition 63, which would establish English as the state's official language, in next month's election. Some states have already passed similar measures and others are making plans to propose such laws.

For Latinos, a growing divide. David Whitman, *U.S. News & World Report* 103:47–9 Ag 10 '87

America's Hispanics, who now account for 7 percent of the population, are failing to achieve the "good life" of the middle class and acceptance into the social mainstream. A recent study shows that the number of Hispanics living in poverty is climbing, as is the number of Hispanic children who attend segregated schools. Language plays a major role in the problems of the immigrants: content to speak Spanish in the barrios, many Latinos have found that their English-language skills aren't adequate in today's increasingly technological job market. As a result, they must usually settle for low-paying, dead-end work. Hispanics view the movement to make English the official language in many states a hindrance to their progress. Some groups, notably the Cubans who fled to Miami, have done well economically, but Latinos in general lack the influence and political clout that could improve their lot.

Less Yiddish, more Tagalog *U.S. News & World Report* 114:16 My 10 '93

A massive influx of immigrants from Asia and Latin America caused the total number of U.S. residents who speak a language other than English to jump by more than a third to nearly 32 million in the 1980s, according to a new Census Bureau survey. Fears that America may be lacking a common language are unfounded, however; the census also reports that 4 out of every 5 people who use a foreign language at home also speak English "well" or "very well."